Dear

MADAM

PRESIDENT

Dear

MADAM

PRESIDENT

★

An Open Letter to the Women
— *Who Will* —
Run the World

JENNIFER PALMIERI

GRAND CENTRAL
PUBLISHING

NEW YORK   BOSTON

Grand Central Publishing
Hachette Book Group
1290 Avenue of the Americas, New York, NY 10104
grandcentralpublishing.com
twitter.com/grandcentralpub

First Edition: March 2018

Grand Central Publishing is a division of Hachette Book Group, Inc. The Grand Central Publishing name and logo is a trademark of Hachette Book Group, Inc.

The publisher is not responsible for websites (or their content) that are not owned by the publisher.

The Hachette Speakers Bureau provides a wide range of authors for speaking events. To find out more, go to www.hachettespeakersbureau.com or call (866) 376-6591.

LCCN: 2017963453

ISBNs: 978-1-5387-1345-7 (hardcover), 978-1-5387-1352-5 (large print hardcover), 978-1-5387-1344-0 (ebook)

Printed in the United States of America

LSC-C

10 9 8 7 6 5 4 3 2

For my sister Dana; my friend
Elizabeth; my hero Hillary;
my mother, Nancy; and
you, our first "Madam President"

CONTENTS

Contents

Dear

MADAM

PRESIDENT

★

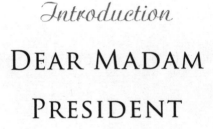

Introduction

DEAR MADAM
PRESIDENT

★

Chart your own path.

*D*ear Madam President:

I am not even sure who you are. Are you, at this moment, sitting on Capitol Hill or in a state house? Are you a young teacher in Maryland wondering if you should run for something? Are you a volunteer mentoring students on the west side of Chicago? Are you browsing through a bookstore in Atlanta, wholly unaware of what your future holds? I don't know if you are a Democrat or Republican or something else, I just

3

know that you are out there somewhere. And you need this book.

I wasn't sure how to address you in this letter. Doesn't *madam* suggest you are married? Are we still going to define women—the first woman president, no less—by relation to a man? I could go with a gender-neutral salutation of "Dear President." It doesn't matter if you are a man or a woman, so long as you can do the job.

Bullshit.

It matters.

And you are going to be different. You will bring an entirely new perspective to the office. You will expand our nation's comprehension of what it means to be a leader. In its best moments, your presidency will give us a more fully realized sense of leadership—one that combines the best qualities of women and men.

There will be many challenges. World and congressional leaders will test you. America will judge you differently than it did your predecessors. People will scrutinize you, your ambitions, your choice of clothes. You are a unique individual, yet you will be expected to represent every woman. Be conscious of it, but keep a positive attitude. It doesn't mean everyone who doubts you is sexist. We inherited this world, with all its flaws. We didn't create it. All of us are trying to adapt and grow.

Given all the gains women have made in the last one hundred years, having a woman president may not seem like that big of a deal. It is. Step back and look at it from the arc of human history. It is still a revolutionary concept for a woman to be in charge. All of our models for a person in power, and certainly for the American president, are based on men. Our founding documents, our theories of leadership and governing, were all written by men, for men. It is time we reimagined leadership roles for women and men both. You will do that for us. You will chart a new course.

When I first joined Hillary Clinton's 2016

presidential campaign, I had a grave misconception about the task before us. Simply put, I didn't think it mattered that Hillary Clinton was a woman. I just thought she was the best person for the job. I didn't see all the complexities inherent in the task of electing the first woman president. Worse, I didn't see the new possibilities having a woman in the Oval Office would open up. We actually set out to prove that it *didn't matter* that Hillary Clinton was a woman. And we did. We showed that this woman could do the job of president as it had been done by every man before her—reducing her to a female facsimile of the qualities we expect to see in a male president.

But I now see that path robbed Hillary of something very valuable. Some measure of her own humanity, some of the qualities that were unique to her. Qualities we may not find in a male president. Qualities *you* will bring to the Oval Office that will add a new dimension to what we imagine when we think of our nation's leader.

Women of the baby boomer generation faced these same constraints in all professions. There was no other blueprint to work from other than to show that a woman could do the job as it had always been done, by a man. *Follow our model, be tough, prove yourself by the standards we set.* You weren't even supposed to look like a woman. *Dress like a man's version of a woman. Our eyes can handle that.* Think of how Patti Smith, Joan Jett, and Pat Benatar, women pioneers in rock music, presented themselves to the world: leather, black blazers, denim. Our eyes accepted them as women tough enough to take on a role meant for a man.

Woman with a guitar. Woman with a gavel. Woman with a podium. Woman with an oval-shaped office. Women with objects of power. It has taken time for our eyes to adjust to them.

Depending on how you keep score, a woman already has won an election for president. Hillary did that. She showed that a woman can win, even when she plays by the rules of the game as established by men. And she won with half of her humanity tied behind her back.

You won't have to do that. You will still have a harder time than you should on the campaign trail. Getting the job will be harder for you than actually doing the job. (You will be great at the job, by the way.) But you will face easier terrain than the last woman did. This time our eyes will be more accustomed to the sight of a woman standing behind the podium center stage at the convention. Our ears more attuned to a woman's raised voice projecting—not shouting—into the crowd. Our sensibilities adjusted to focus on what she will do with the job, not question why she wants it.

So, no gender-neutral moniker for you. You shall be Madam President. Let's celebrate the fact that you are a woman.

I have always thought that I could do any job a man can do just as well as him. Only recently have I come to realize that I don't want to. I want to do the job the best way I can do it, not the way he would. That's what this letter is about—how women can lead in a new way. How we can create a new model of leadership in our own image, not a man's.

You are preparing to lead our nation. Whatever you do to ensure that your voice is heard or that your position prevails, you are doing it in the service of our country. You don't see it as attempting to aggrandize yourself or being pushy. You certainly aren't going to wait to be asked for your view; you are going to assert yourself. If you didn't, you wouldn't be doing your job; you wouldn't be giving the country its due. That's an approach all women should adopt.

I build on lessons I learned from my own life, where I was able to see President Barack Obama bring a new empathy to the Oval Office; from watching women like Hillary, Elizabeth Edwards, and my sister Dana Drago refuse to be defeated, even when the world told them they had lost; from mentors along the way who taught me the value of my own voice.

I will start with one hopeful lesson I learned on Thursday, November 10, 2016, a day after the world learned the outcome of the 2016 American presidential elections. I walked out of our campaign headquarters that night, still dazed from our loss, and encountered a large group of schoolchildren waiting outside for the Hillary campaign staff in the Brooklyn night. They were carrying signs and had covered the sidewalks in front of the building with hopeful messages written in chalk. WE ALL BELONG HERE. RISE UP. DO THE MOST GOOD. I felt a glimmer of optimism. For the rest of their lives, these kids would remember the night their parents brought them to Hillary's headquarters to cheer on the staff.

I remembered those kids two months later when millions of women across America, in communities from Anchorage, Alaska, to Washington, DC, showed up to make their presence known and voices heard as part of the Women's March. Women of all persuasions found it to be an empowering moment. Beyond politics, there was a sense among women that we had plateaued and needed to chart a new path if we were to make the progress we wanted and deserved. It was the start of a new chapter in the American story in which women decided that we were no longer following old rules and conventions. We were creating our own game, and going to write, and tell, our own story. This book is for you, our first Madam President, and for all the women in America from all walks of life and all professions who know they are ready to lead.

Chapter One

THE DAY AFTER

★

When the unimaginable
happens, imagine what
else may be possible.

I want to tell you what that day after felt like.

It felt like a movie scene you would never see. The scene where you don't defuse the bomb just in time. The scene where the world explodes.

It is seven a.m. on Wednesday, November 9. I wake up in my room at the Peninsula New York hotel, having gone to sleep two hours before.

What follows?

Silence. A suffocating silence. Like I have been hurled into a black hole. Disconnected from the

15

rest of the world. It doesn't even seem possible to me that I could still speak with the other campaign staff. I imagine that if I picked up my phone to call one of them, it wouldn't work. I imagine each of them also tumbling in space, in isolation, no gravity, no orientation.

This much I can process: I feel fear. Free-floating fear. It's not attached to anything specific yet. Just fear. Also, this: a yearning—not a hope, because I can feel no hope on this day—but a yearning that this new world America is entering won't be as bad as we predicted. And failure. We failed. It was on us to save America and we let her blow up. I recall President Obama pointing at me in jest just thirty-six hours earlier as he left the Philadelphia rally on Monday night, saying, "Do not mess this up!" "We got it, we got it," I replied. A different universe. A different lifetime. One I desperately want to get back to. One in which I understood how the world operated, where certain things were set in stone.

Oh, God. Springsteen sang about that in Philadelphia, too. He sang "Long Walk Home." It assures us that the "flag flying over the courthouse means certain things are set in stone." I no longer know that to be true. Nothing feels set in stone now.

I decide to give hope a try. *Maybe this isn't the end*, I tell myself. Given how hard the rest of the campaign was, it would make sense that Hillary would not win outright on election night. Maybe this is just another near-death experience. A really scary one. Maybe we will win on recounts. Or fight it out in the electoral college and win there. Right. Winning on November 8 would be too easy. This campaign is going to have to go all the way to December 19 and win in the electoral college. Another five grueling weeks of campaigning in overtime. Then we'll look back on this bleak Wednesday when we got a glimpse of what life would be like in the dark, parallel universe where Donald Trump actually won, and we'll laugh. "Remember how unfathomably *awful* that Wednesday morning felt?"

I try to get myself to believe in that possibility. Later, I'll be able to put enough stock in the theory to act on it. I will push for recounts and to fight it out in the electoral college. But I don't feel real hope. The new postexplosion world I find myself in may be surreal, but it seems permanent to me.

I think of Hillary. Devastation. I think of her and all I can feel is devastation. *She will be the least surprised that this happened.* She came into this race with some reluctance. More than anyone would have imagined. She felt unease throughout the campaign, and we all kept telling her it would be fine. And now she suffers this. Infinitely worse than 2008. I don't feel like we failed her so much as we kidded ourselves into thinking all that we faced was manageable. She could feel what was happening, all the forces—seen and unseen, cosmic and earthly—that were lining up against her.

As soon as these thoughts of Hillary enter my

mind, I shunt them aside. I am in a new world and don't feel like I know how to process emotion yet. I think of my sister Dana. She's in Dallas, on her path to passing. My other sisters are with her: Lisa, Beth, and our new sister, Misty. Misty is Dana's best friend in Dallas and has become her committed caretaker. Four nights before, while I was talking with Sara Latham, who had been managing the campaign transition for us, on how we would staff the communications team, text messages from Beth came in saying—she was sorry to have to tell me this, she knew it was really bad timing—but the doctors thought that Dana could die that weekend and I needed to call her that night to say goodbye. I did. From Hillary's hold room backstage in Cleveland at the Beyoncé and Jay-Z concert. It wasn't the first time I had said goodbye to someone who wasn't long for this earth. I had done the same with Elizabeth Edwards in her bedroom in Chapel Hill six years prior. You have to shout to be heard. I shouted that I loved her and was proud to be her "big little sister." Dana was older, but a little shorter and always much thinner than me.

Lisa, my second-oldest sister, told me on Friday night that even though the doctors thought death was imminent, she bet Dana would make it to Election Day. I agreed. Now it's Wednesday morning and she's still alive.

For the last four days, I struggled to keep everything compartmentalized. Dana went in one compartment. Though those final days on the campaign trail were packed, I found time each day to duck into a church, or go on a walk, or find some moment to commune with her. The doctors recommended that. They said it aided her path. The other compartment held the campaign. There was plenty of anxiety in that part of my head, too.

I woke up feeling terrible on Tuesday, Election Day. An overwhelming sense of unease. It's hard to separate what part of the pall was from Dana and what was caused by the end of the campaign. But I know that even if Dana had been healthy and happily buzzing about Dallas at that very moment, I would still have felt terrible that day. I also know the unease wasn't a premonition of the loss that was to come. Whatever I felt on November 8 was part of life in the old world. It has little bearing on this new one.

My Election Day unease had two sources. One was the stress and anxiety I had fought to suppress for the whole campaign, demanding its due. The second was that as much as I wanted and desperately needed the campaign to end, it had given me a nearly all-consuming purpose, and I feared the void the end would create. The void that came at the end of the 2004 presidential campaign, which had consumed nearly two years of my life, was filled by a crushing depression it took me a year and a lot of hard work to emerge from. This time I wasn't just coming off of twenty months of the most grueling—no—the most *harrowing* campaign on record. My time on the campaign trail was preceded by three years in the Obama White House. And I wasn't facing just the end of a campaign but also the imminent death of my sister.

The anxiety and unease I felt had been lurking for the last week. By Monday, they had won out. I couldn't enjoy Monday night at all, even with all the spectacular trappings of the Obamas, Springsteen, Jon Bon Jovi, Lady Gaga, and Obama and Clinton staff there to enjoy the final rallies. *Enjoy this last night,* I told myself. *Isn't this what you have worked so hard for?* The answer had to be *No, it is not.* All of "this" was for Hillary, and I hoped she was able to enjoy it.

I knew that whatever happened Tuesday night—and I fully imagined a celebration—was to be Hillary's painstakingly hard-earned glory. I knew I would find no value in it for me. I knew whatever satisfaction I was to derive from the effort I put into the campaign, I'd already experienced on Friday morning in Pittsburgh.

When we landed in Pittsburgh, I was told we had a long motorcade ride from the airport to Heinz Field, where our event was. Excellent. Thirty-five minutes of near solitude. Rock star hairstylist Isabelle Goetz, rock star makeup artist Barbara Lacy, and I headed to Staff Van 3. You have to be a real veteran of motorcades to understand the virtues of Staff Van 3. Isabelle, Barbara, and I are such veterans. Staff Van 3 is never as crowded as the other two vans, and even though it is three cars behind Hillary, riders in Staff Van 3 are best positioned to catch up to her when the motorcade stops. Because what matters most in your ability to get where you need to be is the ability to get out of the van fast.

It was just the three of us in the van. We each had our own row. I decided that on this final Friday of the campaign, I was due thirty-five minutes of uninterrupted time to listen to my favorite playlist of the moment, "Staff Walk On." The "Staff Walk On" playlist was a concept Nick Merrill, our traveling press secretary, and I came up with one plane ride a couple of weeks back. It consists of songs that typified the staff's experience on the trail. It has songs like Queen's "Under Pressure," Jason Isbell's "24 Frames," Tift Merritt's "Engine to Turn," Springsteen's "Take 'Em As They Come" and even the hopeful "Amongst the Waves" by Pearl Jam.

It was a sparkling fall day and a beautiful drive alongside the Allegheny River into Pittsburgh. I looked out the window. Ignored the emails and texts. Replayed "Amongst the Waves" a few times in a row. I took the time to really savor these moments. I expected we would win and didn't yet know about Dana's decline. There were reasons to believe I would enjoy other moments of celebration. But I also knew that the moments in which you can feel joy at the end of a long hard effort are fleeting and I needed to take advantage of this one. The gratifying moment isn't likely to be the official moment of victory when your candidate wins.

The gratifying moment is simply the one in which your own mind decides to let you believe you have done your best and your effort has mattered. That is my reward. Because what I have learned about myself is that while I welcome accolades and celebrations like anyone else, I don't derive a sense of accomplishment from them. That can only come from myself. So, no, those moments on Monday night and what I hoped to see on Election Night weren't the ones I had worked so hard for. It was this one. Those moments in that van in Pittsburgh were to be the last sense of well-being I would have for many months.

When I left the Obama White House to join the Clinton campaign as her communications director, I thought that Hillary would win, but I didn't think I would look to join the White House after the campaign. I had twelve years there already working for President Clinton and President Obama and figured I should take a break. In the closing days of the campaign, Hillary talked to me about coming to work at the White House if she won. We never landed on anything definitive, but I probably would have done it. I wouldn't have felt great about it, though. It would have felt like holding on to a crutch, like I was scared to face who I was without a White House title or a candidate attached to my name.

And now, I face a loss on Wednesday morning. The thing I didn't worry about. The thing I was not capable of worrying about because it was unimaginable to me. Intellectually, I knew it was possible to lose. Our own polling in the closing weeks showed a one-in-four and sometimes a one-in-three chance of that. But my gut and my heart saw the very fact that the campaign was so hard as some sort of karmic insurance that we would win. The harder it got, the surer I was that our effort to ward off a dangerous presidency would be rewarded. What seemed unimaginable to me was that we would put Hillary through so much hell, that we ourselves could endure such a grueling campaign, only to lose to Donald Trump. That every moment we participated in during the campaign was a small part we were each playing in our role to make Donald Trump the next president of these United States. That's what I couldn't imagine would happen.

And yet it did. So I enter this new world. Where every day I live with having to watch someone be hurt because of the win we failed to secure. Where the unimaginable happens every day.

Sometimes, in my new life, I will go to text someone and find that the last message I have from them is from election night.

2:43 a.m., Wednesday, November 9: Hey. Hope you are good. Has HRC called to concede?

It's always a jolt. It doesn't seem as if it should be possible for texts from an old universe to exist in today's world. Shouldn't they have been destroyed in the explosion?

Evidently, there was to be some mercy in this new life I began that Wednesday, because, despite what had been expected, Dana Drago was still in it. I had a feeling on that morning, which turned out to be true, that she wasn't going to die soon. She would not recover, of course. You don't recover from early-onset Alzheimer's—not yet. But I no longer felt that I had to race to Dallas to say goodbye in person. I had planned to go on Thursday. I told my husband, Jim, Wednesday morning that I wanted to move my flight to Saturday. I felt like I had more time, and I needed more time.

Hillary loses, Dana persists. You never really know what is going to happen. There is so little within your control. But since we live in a world where the unimaginable is suddenly possible, we need to seize on that by imagining what else might be possible now that seemed unimaginable before.

During the campaign, I spent a good part of

my life on the Northeast Regional Amtrak line, going from New York to my home station in Baltimore. After a long break, I took the train again in the summer of 2017. The Northeast Regional has an unmistakable scent. If you take the Regional, you know the scent I am talking about. It hit me as soon as the doors to the train opened. It smelled like 2016. Homesickness washed over me. I sat down and thought for a while, trying to understand what it was that I actually missed.

I was surprised to find that I really didn't want to go back to my pre-election life. I wasn't entirely comfortable in this new world, but I somehow felt more solid in it. I had survived the unimaginable. Another casualty of the explosion was my anxiety about what my value would be now that the campaign was over. It disappeared the night of November 8 and never came back. I am embarrassed that it took this devastation for me to see what else was possible for me.

Sitting there on the Amtrak, I found that even

though we lost, the memory of my drive in Pittsburgh still gave me a sense of satisfaction.

I did the very best I could in the campaign and put all my heart and soul into it. I kept faith with my candidate and fellow staff and we stuck together through both the campaign and the brutal aftermath when critics—who weren't there and didn't live through what we did—sought to tear us down.

I realized that after the trappings of the West Wing and campaigns and my own expectations of how life is supposed to go are stripped away, all I really need to have value is to put my very best effort into something that matters.

I decided the prickle of homesickness I felt was actually for the confidence I used to have that I knew how things will turn out. I miss my bearings. They were more central to my well-being than I had realized.

I think a lot of women feel that way and initially viewed the uncertain post–November 9 world with unease. We had lived our lives playing by a certain set of rules, and they had failed us. We didn't know what to make of it at first. Could it be that women are meant to go only so far in the world? No, that can't be it. Women haven't plateaued; it is the rules we were playing by that are outdated. We are learning to appreciate that with this uncertainty comes an empowering new sense of possibility. I look around at all that women are doing in America today and I am inspired. Women aren't just running for office in record numbers, they are winning in record numbers, too. In the worlds of art, politics, and business, women aren't following anyone's rules— they are creating their own game.

So you see, Madam President, having survived that unprecedented scene in the movie where the world exploded after all, we can now write our own happy ending. From now on, we will decide what is possible for us. This movie ends with women running the world.

Chapter Two

MOVE FORWARD, DRAW FIRE

★

Brace yourself: Nothing draws fire like a woman moving forward.

*I*t's the afternoon of Wednesday, November 9. We are at the New Yorker hotel and Hillary has just finished her concession speech. I decide to just nod and smile wistfully when supporters and reporters, men and women alike, laud it. "Where was *this Hillary* during the campaign?" they lament. "Why didn't we see this side of her when it mattered?"

Yes, I'm sure you loved her concession speech, I thought. *Because that's what you think is acceptable for a woman to do—concede.*

Had I never left the Obama White House to be part of the campaign, I am sure I would have asked the same question. I probably would have printed out the transcript of her remarks and pored over them, trying to isolate the essence of what made this speech so much more appealing than anything she had said during the campaign. And I wouldn't have found it. Because I needed to have the experience of working for a female presidential candidate to understand why we liked "this Hillary" so much better than "candidate Hillary." Fundamentally it wasn't about the words she used in her concession speech but what she represented. She was no longer a woman pushing to be president. She was a gracious loser putting the needs of her country above her own. That is a role we are comfortable seeing a woman in, even if that woman is Hillary Clinton. It was the role of Hillary as an ambitious candidate that troubled us.

We think a woman shines brightest when she

is selflessly putting others' interests above her own. It is more flattering than seeking her own spotlight.

I have to tell you that when I first joined Hillary's campaign, I didn't think it was going to be that hard or even that big of a deal to elect the first woman president. I thought it would be a tough campaign because Democrats were going for a third term and there's all this "stuff" that seems to hang around Hillary that makes every endeavor she undertakes more difficult for her than it is for anyone else.

But I didn't think electing the first woman was going to be that hard. We had already elected our first black president, and that seemed a more difficult thing to do in America. The way I saw it, women were advancing relatively well in the professional world. I knew I owed a debt of gratitude to the baby boomer women of Hillary's generation who had been the ones to break barriers for women in so many professions, and I appreciated the rocky path they traveled that made the opportunities I had possible. I felt like women were on track now and it would just be a matter of time until one became president.

Suffice to say that after having gone through this campaign, I have a different view. I was wrong. And on two big counts. First, I didn't appreciate what a big deal it was from a historical perspective to elect a woman as president. And while in modern-day America it can feel as if most of us accept that women are equal to men, the women's rights movement is a relatively new phenomenon in our country. Consider this: Hillary Clinton's mother was born on the day Congress took final action to give women the right to vote. Not her great-grandmother, not her grandmother: her mother. That's how new this "women in charge" stuff is in the United States.

Second, and this is the one I feel really bad about, I didn't see as I do now that all this "stuff" that hangs around Hillary stemmed from her being a woman. I didn't think the attacks and criticisms she suffered were fair, mind you. I just thought they were the result of twenty-five years of her and her husband being subjected to political attacks. It's what happens to politicians who survive for a long time. Your haters may not be able to kill you off, but the attacks are going to leave a mark, and they left a mark on Hillary. Of course, she did seem to draw even more ire than her husband. That should have been a clue.

Before I delve into all that happened in the campaign, I want to be clear that while misogyny and sexism were a problem on the campaign trail, I don't believe that everyone who voted against Hillary did so for sexist reasons. If I don't make that clear at the outset, you might come away with the wrong lessons from the stories I have to share from 2016. Nor do I think the people who thought her concession speech was her best speech are sexists. I liked the concession speech, too. But I do believe we encountered an unconscious but pervasive gender bias that held Hillary back in many ways. I think it's that subtle gender bias that made people find her so vexing. I think it comes from her being someone who pushed the boundaries of roles held by women for forty years.

"Move forward, draw fire." That's a joke two of the Secret Service agents on Hillary's detail would say to each other when they would have to manage an internal bureaucratic disagreement. "Guess we only have one option left," they would joke. "Move forward, draw fire." It always made me laugh. I found it to be true on the campaign side of the operation, too. "Yep," I would say. "Sometimes that's the only way." It's not an optimal political strategy. It would be better to just move forward. But it's rare in politics that an offensive move doesn't come with some collateral damage. You have to be comfortable with that. Women are particularly uneasy with drawing fire.

Which is too bad. Because nothing draws fire like a woman moving forward.

★

In a sentence, I think that's what happened to Hillary and why so many people didn't like her or trust her. She has been moving forward and drawing fire for forty years. Brace yourself, Madam President. You, too, will get quite a bit of incoming.

Since Hillary Clinton first delivered her student commencement speech at Wellesley and landed on the cover of *Life* magazine as the female face of the baby boomer generation, she has been a generationally challenging figure. She was the "lady lawyer" married to the governor who hadn't taken her husband's name and made more money than he did. Next, she was the first major presidential candidate's wife who had her own career and didn't "stay home to bake cookies." She was the first First Lady who worked in the West

Wing and took on the touchiest of touchy political issues: health care. She was the first woman to run for Senate, run for president, become secretary of state, and run for president again.

She was constantly stepping outside the confines of the box in which women had always operated. She was always confounding us. Not because we all wanted to keep women in a small box, but because there was no model we could compare her to; she didn't make sense to us. Looking at all this through today's lens, none of what she did may seem revolutionary. But it sure made a lot of people uncomfortable in real time. Forty years later there still isn't a model you can compare Hillary Clinton to, and many people still struggle to make sense of her. Even with all the gains women have made across the board, Hillary's life experiences are without parallel. I think that makes it hard for people to relate to her.

And yet most Americans did think Hillary

Clinton could do the job of president. A majority of voters in 2016 were ready to accept a woman in charge, and that's important progress to be celebrated. The hurdle she never quite surmounted was having us all accept that it's okay for a woman to have the *ambition to want to be in charge*. It's that ambition part where Hillary ran into trouble. No male candidate has ever had to hide his ambition to get elected—after all, there are few goals more ambitious than becoming president of the United States. So despite her qualifications, Hillary's ambition made voters uneasy, yet it wouldn't have been possible for her to run for office without it. The source of that unease is the same unconscious gender bias that inspired the disturbing refrain we heard throughout 2016: "I am fine with a woman being president, just not *this* woman."

If Hillary had won, I think people would have liked her as president. It would have been a difficult existence for her. She would have been hounded by a Republican-controlled Congress from day one. But she is used to that and would have dug in and figured out a way to get the job done. I believe her favorability rating would have risen in office, even though that was not the case with most of her predecessors. Typically, our presidents are most popular when they are candidates. Their popularity drops once they are in office and constrained by the duties of the job. But people seem to like female elected officials once they are in office. That's what happened to Hillary when she became a senator. Once she was in office, she was just doing the job voters gave her permission to do. That's no longer confounding. That's a woman fulfilling her responsibilities. We expect a woman will do a good job.

When Hillary first started the 2016 campaign, she sought out the advice of women academics and researchers who have done a lot of work looking at the issue of women and ambition. After listening to them and others, our polling team advised us that Hillary's ambition needed to be expressed in terms of her desire to serve others. Otherwise, her campaign to be president was off-putting to people. Our culture still tends to characterize ambitious women as pushy, conniving, and selfish. This is not unique to politics—it's true for women in any walk of life. Hillary's ambition to be president could not be about her. She had to be in the race to help others. "In service to others" was a mantra constantly drilled into our heads. We would present her accomplishments as things she had done "in service to others," and what she sought to do as president as being "in service to others." Similarly, our polling showed that Hillary's most popular attribute with voters was that she had been willing to go to work for President Obama, the man she lost to in 2008. *"See?! Her ambition really is about serving others!"*

It was tough making people feel comfortable with Hillary's candidacy, so I was grateful that we had hit upon an attribute of hers that voters embraced. Still, I found it disconcerting that people didn't appreciate the outstanding job she did as secretary of state so much as they approved of her going to work for "the man who beat her."

She did want to be president to help people, so I didn't have a big problem with the "in service to others" mantra. But it was a little disheartening. You may be surprised to hear that Hillary fully embraced "in service to others." I am not sure she loved it, but she knew she wasn't going to change historic sensibilities about women's roles in the span of one campaign. She needed to meet voters where they were and was glad for the advice on how best to do it.

Madam President, the fact that you have been elected means voters have moved a little farther down the road since the days of Hillary's campaign. But whatever resistance persists toward women seeking power, you will have an easier time pursuing your own goals because of the work Hillary did tilling that same soil. All women with big dreams and ambitions will.

One thing our campaign was never able to move beyond was the vexing issue of Hillary's emails. I think it was that unease people felt about Hillary's motivations as a woman seeking power that made it impossible for us to ever fully put this matter to bed. I have weathered a lot of political crises, but never encountered one quite like this. It was a box we could never get out of.

I found the summer of 2015, when we were really drowning in email stories, to be the most difficult time of the whole campaign. We were trying to decipher—and I use that word quite literally—what was really behind the uproar the email story caused and what we could do to move beyond it. The press's goalposts for the questions she needed to address were always moving. First, we had to establish that using personal email was legal. We established that. To this day, no one is satisfied with our answer. Next the press says, "She needs to explain why she used a personal email account." She explained. It's not good enough. "No, tell us why she *really* did it," they would say to me. Next it was "She needs to admit it was a mistake." She says it was a mistake. That's not good enough, either.

After many painful conversations on the matter, we finally decided in late August 2015 that Hillary would do a series of interviews where she could answer more questions about emails, with the hope of putting the matter behind us as we headed into the fall. There was plenty of reason to doubt this plan would succeed. She had answered dozens of questions about emails before to no effect.

At the beginning of Labor Day weekend, she did an interview. Hillary said it had been a mistake to use a personal email account. The reporter then asked her if she thought she owed the American people an apology. *An apology to the American people?* I thought. *For what?*

In all the hours of torturous discussions we had among ourselves, painstakingly going over every question that could possibly arise in any interview, the question of whether she needed to apologize had not occurred to us. Whatever harm had come from the emails, Hillary—and not the American people—bore the brunt of it. Thankfully, the American people weren't an injured party here. I didn't begrudge the asking of the question. It wasn't meant to be a "gotcha," I think she meant it sincerely and was just doing a thorough interview.

Still, my heart sank when I heard the question. I knew that once the issue of whether Hillary needed to apologize had been raised, we were never going to be able to move on until she did. The press coverage would obsess over when Clinton would apologize. *It's day three—where's the apology?* After the interview, we all talked about how to deal with the apology question. Hillary was not happy about it but saw the same reality we all did, so she apologized in an interview with ABC'S David Muir. It still wasn't enough.

That's when it all became clear: *They don't want her to apologize. They want her to confess to a crime she didn't commit. There's nothing she can say that will satisfy them.*

Madam President, I believe this to my very core: If it weren't her emails, it would have been something else. Another issue equally trivial and irrelevant for which Hillary would have been tortured. Because underneath all the questions about wiping servers and deleting emails lay the fundamental truth that what all of this was really about was that there was something about Hillary Clinton folks just didn't trust. And that something was an intelligent, capable, ambitious woman in a position of power.

TSAHIJDL. Get to know it. Whether you are running for president or any woman who challenges the status quo. "There's something about her I just don't like." And its sister complaint: "There's something about her I just don't trust." It's what people said about her twenty-five years ago during her husband's 1992 presidential campaign. Before Travelgate, before Whitewater, before Hillarycare, before Benghazi, before emails.

Madam President, look at all she encountered as a presidential candidate. All the gauntlets she had to run—from being the first presidential candidate ever called to testify before Congress (and earning the record for longest congressional testimony ever while doing it) to being the first candidate for the American presidency targeted by a foreign power. This was not the normal vetting process a presidential candidate goes through. Some larger force was at work here.

Flying back from Florida on October 29, 2016, the day after the infamous Comey letter came out, I joked with Hillary about what seemed to be her ever-growing number of opponents. It felt like we had four men running against us—Donald Trump, Vladimir Putin, Julian Assange, and Jim Comey. I don't believe it is a coincidence that the first woman nominee of a major party ended up being hounded by four men, all taking actions that would influence the campaign in ways never before seen in our country's history. Maybe that's just how presidential campaigns are in the twenty-first century. Or maybe there was just something about her the four of them didn't like.

Putin was no fan of President Obama, but he reserved a special ire for Hillary, the woman who dared to challenge the legitimacy of the 2011 Russian elections when she was secretary of state. Julian Assange had a long-held animosity for her, too, going back to WikiLeaks' foray into the State Department's cables when Hillary was secretary of state. As for Jim Comey, when he sent that letter about additional emails to the Hill, he went out of his way to break precedent, despite claiming that his overriding imperative when it came to managing the Clinton email investigation was to follow standard FBI practice at all times. I know he doesn't see it that way, but obviously there was something about her case that drove him to ignore precedent and take an extraordinary step that may well have cost Hillary the election.

As for Donald Trump, is it a coincidence that the first woman nominee of a major party lost a presidential election to a misogynist? I have my doubts. There were times in the closing weeks when the campaign felt less like a presidential run and more like a primal battle for survival. Between the accusations of sexual harassment and assault against Trump failing to dampen the enthusiasm of his supporters, the creepy "lock her up" rallies, Putin's Russian email leaks, Comey's letters, and Trump threatening that he might not accept the results of the election if Hillary actually won, it was a darkly surreal phase during which I literally had to pause every now and then to confirm that I wasn't dreaming.

Earlier in the summer, Hillary, Senator Tim Kaine, his wife, Anne Holton, and I laughed over the absurdities we encountered in the campaign, talking on our bus one morning in Harrisburg,

Pennsylvania. I told them the campaign felt like a Batman movie version of a presidential campaign—Christopher Nolan–style. Both candidates were from Gotham. Trump was our lead villain but had help from side characters like Putin and Assange. We had other characters who, like Catwoman, were sometimes on our side, sometimes not. I put Comey in this category. President Obama was Commissioner Gordon. And the fate of the world hung in the balance.

It was a funny comparison in July. In October, it almost felt too apt to be considered a metaphor. The trail was a scary place.

Emotions were running so high in the country that I feared there was going to be some violence before the election. I even half-jokingly said to Hillary one day in October that it was beginning to feel like we were upsetting some cosmic natural balance by seeking to "upend the patriarchy." I didn't really believe it, of course, but a large part of the country seemed to believe Hillary represented an existential threat to the proper order of things.

I started this chapter by saying I hadn't expected the task of electing our first woman to be as daunting as it was. I should tell you that Hillary did try to warn me. On March 23, 2015, my first day on the campaign staff, Hillary sat me and deputy communications director Kristina Schake down and basically vomited up what it was like to have been her for the past twenty-five years. She wanted us to hear it all so we had an inkling of what we were likely to encounter when representing her to the press and public. She held forth for more than an hour, starting with her husband's campaigns for governor, her belated decision to change her name to Clinton, the turmoil of White House years, ups and downs she had with the press, the times when the public seemed to really hate her and the times they liked her, what happened in each of her campaigns. She didn't have answers for why all this had happened to her, but she wanted us to be aware of it. I remember she told us that she was "just a simple and serious person" and somewhat baffled that she provoked such rage from some quarters.

I laughed at her description of herself as a "simple and serious person," because she is also a warm and very reliable friend who is a lot of fun and brilliant. She is not "just" a simple and serious person, but I know what she means. She is simple in that she is direct. She doesn't have a lot of time for pretense. She is serious in that she really worries about the state of the world and wants to solve problems, not just look like she's trying to solve them. For all the grief Hillary gets about being inauthentic, the truth is that she is terrible at faking it. When someone asks her a question she thinks is stupid, it shows all over her face. You know the look I'm talking about. Other women politicians are much better at hiding their feelings when reacting to an idiotic or sexist question or a dumb idea from a colleague.

Listening to "simple and serious" Hillary describe her experiences was a poignant moment, too. She was as bewildered as anyone by the phenomenon of "Hillary Clinton." It seemed to me that she was as uneasy with some of the wild adulation of her as she was with the attacks because neither reflects an understanding of the person she really is.

A number of women I know and respect think it is a mistake to go back over everything that happened with Hillary in the 2016 campaign. Their view is that it is self-defeating for women to be seen as complaining about how Hillary was treated. I might share their view if I hadn't lived that campaign. We need to understand what happened. We need to make the path easier for all women working to succeed in whatever role they choose. The unease we felt toward Hillary could hold any woman back anywhere.

Madam President, none of us here today created this world where biases about women, particularly women in power, persist. We inherited it. Most of us—women and men alike—are trying to sort it all out. But there remains something that makes a lot of people uneasy about women trying to move forward. Even when you get to the White House, you will continue to draw fire, perhaps more than ever. That's why I wanted to describe to you the resistance we encountered the first time a woman tried to do this. I hope you draw less fire, but whatever happens, don't let anyone stop you from continuing to move forward.

Chapter Three

IN THE ROOM

Speak up—Your voice is needed.

I have been privileged to gain entry to some of the world's most powerful rooms. The Oval Office. The prime minister's study at Chequers in the UK. Number 10 Downing Street. The German chancellor's office in Berlin. The Blue House in Seoul. The Imperial Palace in Tokyo. Even the Kremlin. I am indebted to the generation of women who came before me and fought to secure my place in those rooms when I am in them, and I speak up on their behalf and on behalf of the women who have yet to gain access to them because I don't want the privilege I have been given to go to waste.

On your path, you will have had to fight to gain entry to the series of rooms that will lead you to the Oval Office. Even though it will have been a struggle, I hope you will know that you belong there and that it is your right and duty to speak your mind when you arrive.

In the Clinton White House, I felt privileged to be allowed "in the room." I had many generous mentors there, men and women both, who taught me I belonged there and my voice mattered. I learned to speak up. It was in the Obama White House where I appreciated that it wasn't just my privilege but my responsibility to speak in whatever room I was in. You aren't doing your job if you don't.

★

I was offered the job of deputy communications director for President Obama in the fall of 2011. I was thrilled at the prospect, but I felt some trepidation because I was going to be replacing a friend of mine, Jen Psaki, who not only was a unique talent but had been with the president since early on in the 2008 campaign and was highly respected by him and all the senior staff.

Both Dan Pfeiffer, the communications director, and David Plouffe, President Obama's senior advisor, assured me that I could count on the same level of access and seniority afforded the other Jen P., that I would be treated as senior staff, that I would participate in all the meetings with the president, and so forth. I thought it was a good sign that they were saying all the right things, but I have to admit I didn't really believe them. As my friend and mentor Doug Sosnik, who was a senior advisor for President Clinton, best described it, the West Wing is a game of pickup basketball. Roles and positions matter some, but not a lot. What matters is your ability to jell with the other players and the gumption to get in the middle of the game.

I was confident in my gumption, but not so sure about the jelling part.

Around ten thirty a.m. on my first official day, Dan said, "Okay, let's go. We've got to go to the Oval for media prep." I thought, *Wow, these guys weren't bullshitting me.* This wasn't going to be a job where I'd sit in the outer office outside the Oval and make snide comments about the boys not letting me in the game and then second-guess the decisions they made in the room I wasn't allowed in. This was going to be a job where I was in the Oval and was expected to have the answers for the president of the United States. That's a whole different story.

Here's how President Obama would handle first meetings with new staff: He was very welcoming, particularly when it was someone's first time in a meeting in the Oval Office with him, because he knew that was an incredibly intimidating situation. He was very kind and went out of his way to keep the stress level low and make you feel comfortable so you could do your job better. He was very aware of everyone in the room. At the end of a meeting—whether it be your first one or not—if you had not offered a view, he would most likely ask you specifically what you thought. Usually the people who had not offered a view earlier in the meeting were women.

He could tell if you were distracted, too. I was once in a large budget meeting in the Oval. I wasn't expected to present in this meeting, so I wasn't feeling like I was in the hot seat and therefore wasn't as engaged as I normally would be. I guess that was evident because at one point the president glanced over at me and said, "Look at Jennifer. She is sitting there looking all stressed about some dumb *Politico* article that's getting ready to run and not going to matter when it does." And he was right! I was quite literally at that moment sitting there, worrying about some dumb story *Politico* was doing. "Don't worry about it," he told me. "It's not going to matter." And he was right.

In my first meeting with him, President Obama welcomed me, made me feel comfortable, and asked me what I thought. As my time there went on, I came to appreciate that he didn't ask people what they thought because he wanted to be nice, although he is, or because he wanted the women to feel included, although he did. He asked people what they thought because *he wanted to know what they thought.*

One day I was in a meeting with the president and the staff members present were all women. (This happened on more than one occasion; you can find the photos online.) The president correctly assessed that one of my colleagues was holding back on sharing what she really thought, not believing it was her place to speak on a topic for which she was not directly responsible. "You are in the room. Speak up," he said to her, although I could tell he meant for each of us to heed his words. He was right; we all needed to hear it. "There is no other room." He gestured around at the curved walls of the office. "See? This is it. It's the Oval Office." He wanted us to make the most out of being in the Oval Office and all the power it represented, and he wanted to get the most out of us.

Valerie Jarrett, a senior advisor to the president and someone who became my good friend and mentor, echoed his sentiments to me later. The president isn't being nice when he asks your view; he needs it. None of us who were entrusted to be part of the president's senior staff was there just to do the job assigned to us. We were in the room because of the experience, perspective, and judgment we brought with us, and the president of the United States needed to hear from each of us. What's hard to accept in that moment is that you are that person whose views are worthy of being heard by the president of the United States.

I was in my mid-twenties when I started working in the Clinton White House. In all my eight years of working with President Clinton, not one person was ever able to finish a sentence, including the president himself. Everyone was interrupted, and if you were scared to jump into an argument, you got left behind. I had no problem with that. I jumped right in.

In some ways, I was more fearless in the Clinton White House than in the Obama White House. Under Clinton, I was happy to be the assertive younger woman mouthing off with my views. I wasn't necessarily in the room to express an opinion, I was there to follow up on whatever was decided in the meeting and to get stuff done. But I shared my views anyway. There was no pressure, I wasn't expected to have the answers, and my words didn't carry the weight of consequence. If anyone was going to act on my suggestion, it was on them. But I understood I had the power to be heard.

Another friend and mentor, Evelyn Lieberman, gave me that power. At the time she gave me this advice, she was a deputy press secretary for President Clinton. She eventually became the deputy chief of staff, along with Harold Ickes, under Leon Panetta (two more mentors). Evelyn, who passed away in 2016, was a remarkable force of nature. She commanded so much respect that all of us, including Leon and Harold, called her "Mrs. Lieberman." Everything was her business; her opinion mattered in any forum where she chose to share it. Her advice to me was simply "People take their cue from you." That's it. If you act like you belong in the room, people will believe you do. If you act like your opinion matters, others will, too. Simple, true, empowering, and life-changing advice. It is applicable for all women in every endeavor we undertake.

On my second go-round serving in the White

House, I was a senior staff person. I ran a department. When I weighed in, my words weren't just heard but had consequences. Having a position of power should make you feel more comfortable expressing your view, and yet I found it was harder for me, and I think it was harder for some other women, too.

That's when you have to get over your inhibitions and rise to the challenge to do the job you were hired to do. You can't think of it as reaching the next rung on the ladder of female empowerment—it's simply a matter of doing your job. Granted, when your job is to advise the president of the United States on how our country should handle an issue for which there are only bad choices, it can be scary as hell. It can seem safer to pull back and say nothing.

To overcome self-doubt in these situations, I finally landed on an accommodation that helped me get over myself, and I think it can help other women, too. Instead of mentally running through all the people who could be better than me at the job, I decided to accept that there are a lot of talented people in my field, and that some of them are probably better than me. If they held a nationwide search to find someone to be the White House communications director, they could probably find someone better than me, I allowed myself to conclude.

But not that much better. And I am the one who's in the room now, and I'm here for a reason: to do a job. Moreover, even though it's my job to speak up and I shouldn't consider every word that comes out of my mouth as striking a blow for female empowerment, I do owe a debt of gratitude to all the women who fought for my right to be in this room. So I'll be damned if I don't make the most of it while I'm here.

Madam President, when you gain entry to the Oval Office, I hope you take that same attitude with you. I also hope you are thoughtful about choosing the voices that surround you. The people in your Oval Office should look like the entire country you represent, not just one ethnicity or gender. Every decision you make will be better because of it. And make sure each of them speaks up. They are in the room, they are there for a reason, and their voices are essential.

Chapter Four

NOD LESS, CRY MORE

★

It's your world and you
can cry if you want to.

It's election night, around ten p.m. I am in the small suite on the tenth floor of the Peninsula that has been set up as work space for the staff. My colleague Huma Abedin has sat down next to me to ask me about the latest returns.

"What are you saying?"

"I am saying that there's a very good chance Donald Trump will be the next president of the United States."

Huma nods.

I recognize it.

It is the same nod I gave when Robby Mook, our campaign manager, called me at Hillary's hotel the night of the Iowa caucus—which we were predicted to win by as many as six points—to say he thought, *thought*, we would win but it would be "really, really, really, really, really close" and maybe I should come over to headquarters. The same nod Hillary gave ten days earlier on the plane in Cedar Rapids, when I broke the news that Comey had reopened the email investigation. The same nod I gave when Robby pulled me aside just two hours earlier at the Peninsula to say something was off in a few of the states—well, something was off in almost all of the states.

Huma nods. The way we have throughout the campaign as we absorbed more bad news, processed another mountain we would have to climb. *"We are twenty-two points down in New Hampshire." "We will lose the Wisconsin primary by twenty points." "Her FBI interview will be on July 2." "There's a really awful video of Trump from* Access

Hollywood." "*WikiLeaks just dumped a bunch of Podesta's emails.*" "*It looks like the transcripts of Hillary's Wall Street speeches are out there.*"

I register Huma's reaction to the news that we are likely to lose. Her stoicism is remarkable, but not surprising. Huma nods because it is all she or I know on this campaign. We never permitted ourselves any other kind of reaction to bad news. You don't blanch, you don't panic, you show no emotion. *I can handle this. I can handle anything.*

Men may nod stoically at bad news, too. It's where the practice started, after all. But it is required of the women. People—men and women alike—will watch for your reaction to bad news. *Can she handle this? Is she tough enough?*

There's something else in the nod from a woman. An acquiescence. A need for approval. If this is the hoop, I will jump through it. If I don't nod, if I somehow object, say this is all too hard, then I am not ready for this. And I am ready for anything. It's how successful women in all walks of life—whether they are leading a small family or a large company—behave.

That's how I have operated my whole career, and I was proud of it. No one was tougher than me. I thought it worked great, until dehydration and exhaustion landed me in the hospital one day in late August 2016.

Hillary emailed me as soon as she heard, and I emailed her back and explained what had happened. She responded with an all-caps screed any twelve-year-old girl would be proud to call her own: "OMG. WHERE ARE YOU? WHAT CAN I DO TO HELP? PLEASE DO WHATEVER THE DOCTORS TELL YOU TO DO! YOUR HEALTH IS TOO IMPORTANT!"

They sent me home later that night. I slept for four days and then went back out on the trail. Then a week later, Hillary came down with pneumonia. I forwarded her the screed she sent me and told her to take her own advice. She didn't. I didn't. Like most women. We nod the next time we get some bad news and keep going.

Every woman reading this knows what I am talking about. This nodding is one of the ways women have adapted our behavior to succeed in a man's world. For me and a lot of other women I know, it's a toxic brew of the need to prove we are tough enough to play a man's game combined with a woman's sense of duty. We all feel the need to be a superwoman, which in my experience means being all that society has traditionally expected of women, with what we aspire to do added on to the side.

Men spent centuries building the professional world, devising rules to make sure it was a comfortable place for them and that it was geared toward their particular qualities and skills. Like any good guest, women have looked for clues on how we are to behave in this foreign land. We have tried to understand and follow the local customs. We have intuited that in this world we are to be obliging, calm under pressure, and diligent, and to always keep our emotions in check. Our adaptive skills have served many of us well. But we aren't in a man's world anymore. Now it's our world. And shame on us women if we don't do something to change the way this game is played so that everybody is able to bring their best to the effort. Let's embrace a new way of working that is equally geared toward our own qualities and skills.

What would have happened if at some point in the Clinton campaign I hadn't nodded and absorbed the latest blow, but objected? If I'd said, "That's crazy, we can't let this happen" or "That's crazy, we can't survive that?" Sadly, I have no idea, which is why we have to change. We have no idea what beneficial qualities we might be stifling in ourselves as long as we continue to follow an outdated set of behavioral rules that were designed to permit women to play a niche role in a workplace built for men.

Madam President, I have a suggestion for two

new guidelines all women can adopt in the workplace to make it better suited to our qualities. Let's nod less and cry more.

Crying at work? It's long been considered a workplace sin for women, right? No more. Imagine what would happen if we all showed up to work one day and started bawling—the ultimate female power play! Crying isn't a show of weakness. It's a powerful demonstration of emotion. It's not something you should do constantly, but I don't see the need to fight to hold the tears in the way we do. For women (and at least some men), crying can be a way we express anger or frustration or passion or sadness. We shouldn't mute all of that.

I am a pretty big crier. I am not someone who will sob at work, but I am easily moved to tears when talking about something or someone I care about. Most of the time my eyes will mist and just shine with tears, but no tears fall. If the press was writing about it, I think they would describe it as being "visibly moved." Sometimes, if it is something I really care about, my eyes will shine and my voice will crack, too. That's what happened at Harvard.

The Harvard postmortem is an event built into the campaign process that gives every defeated campaign the opportunity to be gracious losers. Officials from the winning and losing campaigns come together at Harvard for two days of questioning from the press. Harvard records and transcribes all the sessions to be published in a book they dub the "first draft of history" of the campaign.

I understood that the thing you are supposed to do when you lose a presidential election is accept defeat gracefully for the good of your candidate and for the good of your country. You are supposed to take ownership, explain what mistakes you made, and stop criticizing the winner. This is particularly expected of the female staff of the losing campaign. Except I hadn't expected to lose and wasn't sure this was a year when you were supposed to be gracious about it.

I had signed up to go to Harvard earlier in the

fall, when I thought we would win, but my colleagues had to convince me to go after our loss. Not because I can't be a gracious loser in theory, I just couldn't see being gracious to this particular team given the way they had beaten us. I was eventually convinced that we needed to go to defend Hillary—otherwise the press and Trump's team would pummel her. As if losing weren't punishment enough.

Trump was a phenomenon I had never seen before—a president riding into office on a strategy dependent on dividing the country to succeed. In the days preceding the forum, I pictured myself summoning just the right combination of words for this first draft of history that would make clear that the 2016 election was something different. I wanted everyone there to know I would rather lose than win the way Trump did, and that I wasn't embarrassed to have been on the losing side. That as time went on, I would be proud to have been part of the effort to stop Trump.

That's what I imagined I would say, but I knew that I would have to forgo most of what I had composed in my imaginary diatribe. However, I did promise myself at least one moment where I would call out the Trump campaign on race.

I didn't know what to expect from the Trump side. I thought there was a chance that the Trump team, for the sake of their own reputations, would decide to behave like gracious winners. That's not what happened. They gloated. They taunted us for two and a half hours. At first, I sat there glum and relatively mute. We were the losers, after all, and I was waiting for the right question or opening that would give me my opportunity to say my piece. The moment came when Dan Balz of the *Washington Post* asked us how it felt, in both campaigns, when Steve Bannon was hired to be the CEO of the Trump campaign. My colleague Karen Finney started in first, calling the Trump campaign out on their race baiting. Exasperated, frustrated, and angry, I joined in.

All of the imaginary conversation—both what I'd intended to keep in my head and what I thought needed to be said—came flying out of my mouth. And I did not deliver it with just the right combination of words or with the calm, steely resolve I had imagined myself possessing when the moment came. Nope. It was all said through misty eyes with my voice shaking. I was emotional. I really cared about the words I had to say, and they moved me to tears.

After my outburst, the rest of the panel was a blur. I left the room in a hurry with Robby to help him get ready for his own one-on-one televised session with Kellyanne Conway. Then, on my flight out of Logan, there were a number of reporters. One of them called out to me, pointing at her phone and waving her arms. I got it—the story was blowing up.

The Harvard postmortem isn't normally a big news event, but this year was to be different. I landed in DC and my phone buzzed with texts and stories the news outlets had written up on the exchange. It was officially "a thing." The *Washington Post* described it as a "shouting match." *We were not shouting!*, I thought in irritation. The *Post* also said I "choked up." I put the phone down and drove home. My husband was watching Brian Williams on MSNBC and they were playing audio of the panel. *Audio? There's audio of this thing? Who knew?* I listened and winced. Yep. We were shouting. And I did indeed choke up. My voice was shaking.

Three strikes against me—I showed none of the grace losers are supposed to, I accused my opponents of stoking racism, and I cried while I did it. This was going to leave a mark. I couldn't care that night and went to sleep.

A few days later I had a meeting with an acquaintance in DC. "I saw what happened," he said to me. "That kind of thing isn't good for anyone. I guess it was too soon for you."

"It wasn't too soon," I said. "I don't regret it."

I was glad I'd said it. The tears were distracting

for some people, but I was angry and emotional and it all made we want to cry. That couldn't be helped. I couldn't get through it without crying.

Think of all the times you have heard someone say they passed on sharing something that was particularly moving because they didn't think they could get it out without crying. That's a shame. Think of all the incredible things we didn't get to hear because someone was scared we would see them cry. In the aftermath of the Harvard event, I was glad to find out that it didn't matter to me. I spoke the truth about something I really cared about. It was worthwhile.

In the Clinton White House press office, my office was referred to as "the crying room." The press staff endured many stressful days together. People were always welcome to come cry in my office when they needed to let some of the stress out. At least once a day, someone was in there crying. Usually it was a woman. Not always. Men cried in there, too. Sometimes they would want me to hear them out, sometimes they wanted to be left alone to cry. No one I worked with—man or woman—thought anything of it other than that it was a human reaction to the inhumane crush a president and his or her staff endure. No stigma was attached to anyone who had to use the crying room. I certainly used it myself many times. A woman can be both strong and emotional. I am. I am someone who cries when I am moved or frustrated, and I am great in a crisis.

I hope you will see fit to let us see some of your tears, as other presidents have done in recent years. It will be more loaded when our first woman president cries, I don't discount that. But the American public that elects you will already know you are strong, so if you sometimes tear up in public, it may help normalize the practice and make other women less reluctant to cry in the workplace. And make sure your White House has a crying room. It's our world and we should be able to cry in it if we want to.

Chapter Five

KEEP YOUR HEAD (AND YOUR HEART) DURING A STORM

You need both to steer
the ship to safety.

*M*adam President, in the course of my career, I have ridden out more than my share of political storms. I was there for Whitewater, the Clinton impeachment, John Edwards's trial, the HealthCare.gov website crash, the Ebola epidemic, Hillary's emails, Russian hacks and leaks, multiple natural disasters, and foreign policy crises like the Kosovo War and ISIS beheadings. It iss pretty fair to say that I have seen it all, and it is certain that you will encounter many more crises in the Oval Office. Know they can have a very destabilizing effect on a White House if you fail to lead properly. You are going to need to keep both a cool head and a warm heart to steer your ship through the storm.

Everyone gets the "keeping a cool head" part of the equation. You have to lead by example and keep your team calm and focused in a crisis. I have learned from watching President Obama and Hillary Clinton that the best leaders also listen with their hearts in times of crisis. They make sure the people serving them have the moral support they need to get the job done, and they make sure the people they serve are getting the leadership they need, too.

★

It was October 2013. I was the White House communications director and responsible for press around the launch of HealthCare.gov, the website to sign up for health insurance under the Affordable Care Act. It wasn't going well. The website did not work and there was devastating wall-to-wall press coverage of the failure. I saw it as my responsibility to fix it.

On one level, it was kind of a silly crisis. Our national security wasn't threatened. Nor did we face any real health threat, as we did the following fall with the Ebola outbreak. It was simply a website that did not work but eventually would get fixed. Nevertheless, the failure presented a very serious risk to us. The press coverage was relentless and was doing real damage every day to President Obama's standing, the credibility of the health care program, and people's belief in the ability of government to tackle big problems. There was a lot on the line, and I felt enormous pressure to do something to stem the tide of terrible press.

My colleague Tara McGuinness and I spent a lot of time and effort trying to come up with ways to improve the news coverage. We searched for the few people who had gotten the website to work and have them tell their stories. I worked to draw attention to other important work that was happening in the Obama administration. None of it helped. I was searching for a moment that would count as a turning point in the crisis that would successfully move the press off of covering the website and on to other issues. It eluded me.

The team working on health care held daily meetings with President Obama to update him on our progress. At the end of each meeting, Tara and I would tell him our latest plans to try to improve the press around the website. After one meeting, as we got up to leave, the president told Tara and me to stay back. He told us, "I want you to know that I know that the press isn't going to get better until the site actually works." He went on to say, "It's great that you are trying and you should keep at it. But I just want you to know that I know this story isn't going away till we get the website working."

I was grateful that he saw the situation clearly and knew it was not possible for us to generate better press under the current circumstances, and that he had the heart to know that Tara and I needed to hear that from him. It relieved a lot of the stress I had been feeling and gave me the ability to look more clearly at the situation and come up with a realistic plan for how to manage press while the website was being fixed.

We did that by establishing a credible timeline for when the site would be repaired. We would do periodic press calls to update the media on the progress we were making. We set up press visits to the headquarters where the work was being done so there was something for the cameras to film. The team fixing the site hit their marks, we started to regain a bit of credibility, and two months later the site worked. The press moved on to other matters.

★

It was July 2013. The verdict in the Trayvon Martin murder case had recently been handed down and there was tremendous pain and outrage in the African American community over the acquittal of George Zimmerman, the vigilante who had shot and killed the unarmed teenage boy. It was clear that the president's voice was going to be needed to help calm this storm. At the staff level, we had been discussing what he should say in response to the verdict. I thought he needed to talk to the African American community and was working through different options that would be most suitable. We were looking at African American radio shows or maybe a visit to a local boys club so the president could visit with some black teenage boys and let them know they were loved and valued.

The president called me, Valerie Jarrett, and our press secretary, Jay Carney, down to the Oval Office to discuss. When we got there, I asked him if he thought the African American community needed to hear from him. "No," he said,

"I think I need to speak *for them*." He then laid out what he thought needed to be said. He said thirty-five years ago, he could have easily been Trayvon, a seventeen-year-old black boy whose life was cut short because someone was unnerved by the color of his skin. He spoke of experiences he had in his own life of white women crossing the street to avoid him at night or security guards following him around stores to make sure he didn't shoplift. He talked about how he and Mrs. Obama knew if they had sons instead of daughters, they would have to have "the talk" with their sons about going out of their way to steer clear of trouble with the police. The president was sitting in his customary yellow chair on the right side of the fireplace. I sat on the couch facing him and listened as our first black president told us about his own personal journey with racism. Behind his head was a bust of Martin Luther King Jr. and a framed copy of the Emancipation Proclamation. Like any job, working in the West Wing could feel like a grind. You faced an endless stream of crises for which there were no easy solutions— just an unappealing set of bad options from which you sought to make the right choice. Press and political criticism were unending. It could wear you down. But then there were moments like this one, when you know you are witnessing history. I felt profoundly grateful to be in this room and hear him share these stories. I knew I was witnessing history.

The next day, the president went to the White House Press Briefing Room and shared with all of the country what he had told us privately the day before about what it is like to live as a black man in America. It was a remarkable moment. No pollster would have advised him to make a speech like that, but it was something all of the country needed to hear. He had listened with his heart and understood what the people of this country— black and white—needed from their president at that moment.

Hillary has had more than her share of storms to weather. A big one came her way on October 28, 2016, when the news broke that the FBI was reopening the Clinton email investigation. We were flying to Iowa when we learned of the news. Robby, Nick, and I approached Hillary on the plane, preparing to tell her of the shocking development.

"I have something to tell you," I said to her.

"Okay!" she said cheerfully. "What do you have to tell me?"

"It's bad," I reply. "Really bad."

"Okay," she said, turning serious and folding her hands to brace herself for what was coming. After I told her the news, she nodded and then got the slightest wry smile on her face. "You knew we weren't done, didn't you?" I asked.

"Yes, I knew we weren't done," she responded. She knew we weren't going to make it all the way to Election Day without a major new plot twist, and here it was. "All right" she said matter-offactly. "Let's talk about what we are going to do about it."

We discussed putting out a staff-level statement first and decided she should speak publicly to the matter later in the day, after we learned more. This was the worst kind of crisis, the kind in which you have no means of even knowing what you're dealing with. It's not as if the FBI contacted the campaign to explain what was happening. The only information we had was what we heard from the media and what was in the Comey letter. We were flying blind.

The FBI had decided, for whatever reason, to reopen the email investigation. That wasn't a problem we could solve. All we could do was figure out how to address this sudden reappearance of the elephant in the room in such a way that we could then quickly move the press away from the subject and on to issues people cared about. We decided the best course of action was to call on the FBI to tell the public the full details of what it was examining and express our concern about the timing of such a momentous action this close to an election. We did this in a written statement from the campaign and then as part of a press conference by Hillary.

She showed remarkable composure at that press conference and over the course of the next eleven days as we sought to ride out this storm. Behind the scenes, beyond her composure, Hillary showed remarkable heart. By the end of that day in Iowa, we understood that the FBI's new actions on emails were actually related to the case it was pursuing against Huma Abedin's then-husband, Anthony Weiner. It was wrenching to watch the pain this news caused Huma. She was distraught. Hillary and I sat with her in our cabin on the plane as Huma sobbed. "He is going to kill me" was all Huma could manage to say in between sobs. She had been through so much in her marriage and on the campaign and had always managed to stay focused on her job and wear a brave face through whatever crisis she was facing. This was a rare moment when she broke down. I watched as Hillary hugged her and was able to help calm Huma down. On the flight back to New York, Hillary insisted all of us have big ice-cream sundaes in an effort to cheer Huma up. She never said a word of complaint over the course of the next eleven days about the impact the Comey letter was having on her personally. From the moment I came to her with the bad news till Election Day, she maintained an upbeat attitude and kept all of us focused on what we needed to get done. She was a real trouper and used all of her head and heart to steer us.

Looking back, I see that we on the staff should have listened more to what Hillary's heart was telling her during this time. On the staff side, we were watching polls to try to judge how people were taking in the news of the Comey letter. Hillary was listening with her heart, and what it told her was at odds with what her team was advising.

While emails were quite literally the last topic we wanted voters to hear Hillary Clinton talk about barely a week before the election, we initially all agreed she needed to address the issue in her campaign speeches for the first couple of days after the story broke. We knew people would be hearing about emails in the press and wanted to have them hear our side of this story. But after a couple of days, I was convinced it was time for us to move on to other topics. The rest of the campaign team was eager to get back to talking about "issues people care about," and I agreed that we had already said the little bit we were able to say about the FBI and should not continue to give the press footage of Hillary talking about emails. So we stopped addressing it.

Unfortunately, the story stuck around and continued to dominate news coverage of the campaign. Every day, Hillary would ask if we were all sure she shouldn't be talking about the FBI and emails in her remarks. She was uneasy about not addressing it and leaving a vacuum for her opponent and others to fill, even though there was no polling evidence suggesting it was helpful for her to continue to talk about it. In retrospect, I see she was right. But we convinced her it was better for her to not raise the emails and instead to talk about issues that affected people's lives and problems she would solve as president. But no one was hearing her talk about the issues they cared about, because they were still hearing about emails.

Whether or not it would have helped, it was foolish on our part to not continue to proactively address the FBI matter. We should have understood that people would take their cue from the media and continue to care about the emails, and that our attempts to focus attention on anything else would be perceived as avoidance of a painful subject.

It was a mistake, though at the time it was hard to accept that telling Hillary to keep bringing up the emails herself could possibly be the right advice. But I should have seen that, as unappealing as addressing the issue was, it was what voters needed to hear from Hillary at that moment. She got that. It is the same sense President Obama had that told him what the country needed to hear from him about race after the Trayvon Martin case.

Madam President, you are certain to encounter many storms; that cannot be avoided. Listen to both your head and your heart when you are leading in a time of crisis. Keep a cool head and hear the advice of your counselors. Take in all the wisdom their expertise brings them. But also listen to what your heart tells you the people serving you and the people you serve need from you in this crisis. There are times it may be at odds with the advice you are getting. Trust most what your own heart and head tell you to do. They will help you steer the ship to safety.

Chapter Six

EMBRACE YOUR BATTLE
SCARS

Show us what you have been through. It tells us what we can survive.

*A*ll of our presidents age in office. It is practically a national pastime of ours to marvel at the toll the job takes on the face of our presidents. During President Obama's second term, I remember being stunned by photos of him from the 2008 campaign. So young! The Barack Obama from 2008 looked like he could be the son of the man who was president now.

I know all this wear and tear on your face will pose a special challenge for you. You, more than all the men who preceded you, will be judged on your appearance and how attractive you are. I don't expect you will ever stop paying the "pink tax," the additional hour or more required for hair and makeup. Those days are not behind us. No matter your age, you will be judged on your face, weight, clothes, and hair. And no matter how lined your face is or isn't coming into this job, it will age with the job. It will acquire battle scars. I think your battle scars can be a comfort to the rest of us. They will show us what you have endured and tell us what we can survive. I hope you will let them show. I do.

I want my own face to be attractive, but I also want it to tell you something about the life that I have lived. I have had a lot of experiences; I want something to show for them. The first time I noticed wrinkles forming between my eyebrows was during my years in the Clinton White House, and I was happy to see them. I thought the wrinkles told you I had lived through stressful times and gained some wisdom and maturity during them.

Later, I remember seeing a brochure at a spa that told you how you could get rid of the "elevens" between your brows. *My "elevens"?* I thought. *These wrinkles have a name? And I am supposed to get rid of them? But they are so cool!* I decided I was going to let my elevens show. They told a story about myself I wanted the world to see.

I also want the joy and sadness I experienced on my fiftieth birthday to show on my face. My fiftieth birthday was one week after Election Day. I had figured out that there was supposed to be a surprise birthday party for me on Wednesday, November 9. I had gotten emails from friends who missed the "surprise" part of the party invitation and said either that they were excited to celebrate with me or were sorry they couldn't make it. I had not let on to Jim that I knew. On that Wednesday morning, I told him that I'd figured out there was some sort of party and didn't think I could do it and wanted to cancel. I expected he might protest, but he agreed.

It is Tuesday, November 15. I've decided to spend my actual fiftieth birthday in Dana's hospice room at Silverado Turtle Creek Memory Care in Dallas. It is just me and Dana in the room. Beth and Lisa left a few hours ago, after being there for a week. Misty is out running errands. Ingrid Moss, one of Dana's amazingly dedicated and knowledgeable home health caregivers, steps out so I can have time alone with Dana. It is a beautiful day in Dallas. We have the window open to let a slight warm breeze into the room. The autumn sun in Texas is something I delight in. It is just bold enough to leave you feeling warm inside and out. I had planned on leaving Dallas the day before but decided I wanted to be with Dana on my actual birthday. I called Jim from Dana's room on Monday to tell him I was going to stay another day. To my great surprise, Dana hears and understands. "Thank you." They were the only intelligible words she volunteered to me during my final days with her in Dallas. She can still, at times, respond to direct yes-or-no questions. But this "thank you" was something she initiated. A final gift to me.

It soothes her to hear music. I put on "May the Long Time Sun Shine upon You," a favorite song of hers from practicing and teaching yoga. I play it over and over. Then I play music she and I loved together growing up. America. The first gift I remember buying Dana was *History: America's Greatest Hits* for five dollars at the navy exchange in Charleston, South Carolina, in 1977. We listen to it. I move on to Boz Scaggs's *Silk Degrees*, which we listened to a lot when all four sisters were living together in Dana's one-bedroom apartment in Benicia, California, for a few months in 1980. My dad had retired from the navy in April and had started a new job in another town, so all four of us girls lived together while Beth and I finished the school year and Lisa, back for the summer from Clemson, lifeguarded at a nearby pool. Poor Dana. She was twenty-two years old, just graduated from college, had her first real apartment on her own, and had to live there with her three little sisters. I know she had some low moments at the time, but the four of us laughed about it for thirty years after.

Next, I put on Dan Fogelberg, Seals and Crofts, Carole King, Jackson Browne. Eventually, we end up in the modern day and I play Sara Bareilles's "Brave." This has become Dana's anthem, and while she was still able to do so, she had sung it every morning. I sing it for her this time. I text Lisa to tell her what we've been doing. *You were able to get through Brave???* she asks. Me: *Yes. It was sad, but good.*

And it was. There were many excruciatingly difficult moments in Dana's illness from Alzheimer's. But there was never a moment when we felt we had truly lost Dana. You could look in her eyes and see that behind the plaque that built up in her brain and prevented her from understanding and communicating, Dana was still there. I would tell her so. I would look her in the eye and say, "I see you. I see you in there." Most times she would nod back. I could tell it was a comfort to her. In those moments, she was Dana refined—not reduced, but refined to her most essential self. Time was suspended. It could be 2016, it could be 1976. We are sisters, holding hands and feeling the bonds that bind us together over decades and just able to love each other. Those moments in her Dallas room were the most meaningful and joyful that I spent with her, that I ever spent anywhere with anyone.

I say my final goodbye to her and head to the Dallas airport. I decide to take a picture of myself to memorialize my fiftieth birthday and final day with Dana. There's a Shiner Bock in the foreground. You can see the two new important talismans I am wearing—a butterfly necklace my father gave the women in our family in Dana's honor and the small "Love and Kindness" medallion Hillary gave me on the last day of the campaign. In one week I have faced the loss of the most important presidential campaign of my lifetime and saying goodbye to my big sister. You can see the wear and tear of the last year in the photo. There are laugh and sleep-deficit lines around my eyes, smile and frown lines around my mouth. I am okay with them. I decided years ago that I didn't want all that I have lived and learned to be smoothed over. The moments I just spent with Dana are in those lines. What I hope they show to the world is that you can endure a loss like the one my family experienced and find unexpected blessings, joy, and meaning along the way. I hope that is what shows in the slightly sad but warm smile on my face in that photograph.

I have always found older women's faces to be a comfort to me. I look at them and imagine what the lines tell me about all they have lived through. They are our connection to a time most of us can't remember. When I was growing up in the 1970s and '80s, I remember being envious of women who could remember a time from decades before. I imagined that having that long of a memory gave a person ballast and depth. A person who had lived for many decades would know they could trust themselves to handle any situation. I am glad to now be such a person who can remember back decades. Look at my face. It tells you that I was a child in the 1970s. I am your connection to that time. I can tell you the songs that were popular and how we dressed and what the country felt like in that moment. I hope my face, which doesn't just resemble Dana but shows that I lived in the same time as her, is a comfort to my niece and nephews.

I hope that society eases up on the pressure for each of us to look young. I am exhausted by the omnipresent, stifling pressure of *now* I see and feel everywhere. Seeing an older face makes me feel more grounded. There was something before this moment, and there will be something after.

I want to see that in my president's face, too.

Because it's not just the burden of the job I see in the weathered faces of our presidents. I see the love they have for this country, the same way parents carry the love and concern they have for their children in their faces. Embrace your battle scars. They will show us all what you have endured in your life and in this job. They will tell us what we, too, will be able to survive, and how much care and worry you put into this job on our behalf. They will tell us that you have been looking out for us—that our dreams, our challenges, what we have lost and the times we are victorious, all mean something to you.

Chapter Seven

HER STORY

Don't search for your role in his story—Write your own.

The future is female. The past was, too. It's just that no one thought it was important enough to bother writing it all down.

Women have been a vital part of America's history all along. But it's hard to find that presence recorded anywhere. The women who appear in our history books are but a handful. Nor will you find us in the history of our nation's most important writings, our founding documents. The Declaration of Independence, the Bill of Rights, the Constitution, were all written by men (white men, of course). Some women may have had their fingerprints, if not signatures, on these documents, as noted in Cokie Roberts's book *Founding Mothers*. But imagine how those documents— and the country founded upon them—would have been different if women had had an equal say in what was in them. Now multiply that out and consider all the state constitutions, laws, history books, novels, movies, and plays that have been written by men in our country. You can understand how a woman might get the idea her story doesn't matter in America.

Hillary Clinton didn't think her life story was interesting. This is common for women candidates. I got my first hint of the complexities involved in telling her story when we set out to find a suitable place for Hillary to make her formal presidential campaign announcement. It was early on in the spring of 2015. We were meeting in Hillary's offices in midtown Manhattan and reviewing the potential speech sites our advance staff had identified. Of the options presented to us, I thought City College in New York City was the best choice. The diverse background of the students there spoke to the future, and I thought it was a good fit given Hillary's history of advocacy for schools and children. Plus, it had a glass atrium, which was symbolically appealing for a woman looking to break the glass ceiling.

Hillary was skeptical. She told us that she thought she needed to go somewhere that had more of a connection to our country's history. I made a face at that comment because it puzzled me. I told her that she didn't need to do that. That sort of thing was for candidates who weren't already well-known. For example, relative presidential newcomer Senator Marco Rubio, who is the son of Cuban refugees, chose to launch his campaign at Miami's Freedom Tower, where Cuban refugees were first processed after being welcomed into America. It was a smart and inspiring location for him. It was a good way to tell his story.

I didn't think Hillary needed to do that. Wherever she announced would hopefully *become* historic because the first woman president had announced there.

She still thought she should cloak herself in the history of other presidents so Americans would have a way to connect to her. This still did not make sense to me. *Why do we need to connect her to history? Let's tell* her *story.*

That's when I learned that Hillary didn't think she had an interesting story to tell. She said that her husband had a "story" and President Obama had a "story," but she did not. She did not see anything remarkable in her story, no struggle to which Americans could relate. She grew up middle-class and had a mother who had struggled and whose difficulties had inspired Hillary to take up children's causes, but Hillary herself didn't struggle. She was the first person in her family to go to college and then law school. Then she met Bill Clinton and the rest is his story, or history—same thing.

We all liked her husband's story when we first heard it in 1992. He was from a place called Hope and born into a life of struggle. He lost his father before he was even born. He was young and smart, worked hard, pulled himself up by his bootstraps, and rose from small-town America to become president of the United States. That's a story we recognize as part of the American story. We like that. We want the lives of our presidents to reflect the classic elements of the American dream.

President Obama's story was more of a reach for many of us, but we still found something of ourselves that we valued in it. The life story of an African American man named Barack Hussein Obama wasn't one we immediately recognized as part of our own. But he *told*—and represented— a story about America we wanted to hear. He told us that we weren't red states or blue states, we were the *United* States. He was going to bring us hope and change, and his election as our first black president represented the fulfillment of a promise of equality in America. President Barack Obama was an "only in America story" and it made us proud.

But the first woman president? It wasn't part of the American story. All our leaders had been men. Our history—the canon of American stories we treasured and told us who we were—were all based on men. Hillary didn't fit the narrative.

I thought about what Hillary said of her own life, and had to admit she had a point. I am embarrassed to say it now, but when I considered her life story at the time of the campaign, I didn't find it compelling. I didn't see anything remarkable in her upbringing. She had endured struggles as an adult, but they weren't the kind of struggles everyday Americans identified with. Worse, we saw them as distracting. It's not enough for your life to be hard—it has to make sense to us, we have to recognize the struggle, it has to tell us a larger story we want told about

America. It didn't work with her story. There wasn't anything in our history to compare to Hillary. I guess that's what happens to the people who are *making* history. We don't appreciate their value in real time.

We ended up at FDR's Four Freedoms Park for the official announcement. Hillary was happy with it because it positioned her as part of a lineage of Democratic presidents who sought to solve big problems in our country. That was appropriate for her; it was what she wanted to do as president, even if it wasn't her story.

But whatever a woman's story might be, it's hard for her to tell it when her voice isn't heard. It is also hard for her story to be told when people are too busy disliking the sound of her voice to listen to what she is saying. I ran into these problems with Hillary, too.

Throughout the campaign I was bombarded with advice from well-meaning folks who had recommendations for how Hillary could improve her speaking style. It was all contradictory. At first I thought it was me, and that I wasn't understanding the recommendations, but after a while I realized that they just didn't make sense. In one memo a person would argue that she needed to project strength but couldn't be shrill, couldn't ever shout but needed to show passion, couldn't ever look weak but should show more vulnerability. The main advice in each memo was for her to be "authentic." I complained to Hillary one day about how frustrating all of it was. She came up with the best response to this kind of advice. "Tell them," she said, "that you really appreciate the advice but what would really help Hillary is if they could tell you the name of a woman on the world stage who does it exactly right." No one could ever produce a name, of course. When it comes to pleasing the masses in a patriarchal society, women seeking power can't win playing by the old man-centric rules. This is why we should stop expecting to find ourselves reflected in our country's history and models of power, and write our own story.

That's what Hillary decided to do when she wrote her book *What Happened*. It's not what losers normally do. I will admit to having been one of the hand-wringers who worried this would end badly for her. Whenever she has set out to explain herself in the past, whatever she had to say has been processed through some weird reverb and ended up distorted.

This time something different happened. This time she was heard. For sure, there were those who criticized her, particularly right after the book came out, and a lot of people who just seemed to want her to go away. But she didn't care—she knew that was going to happen when she wrote the book. She kept going and eventually her story was heard. In the end, much of the press ended up applauding her candor during her book tour. Predictably, there were a lot of people who lamented that "if only we could have seen *this Hillary* during the campaign, things would have turned out different." That's all bullshit. She was always the same person. We are the ones who perceive her differently in different situations.

We now see her story as interesting. Her book will be valuable to you, too. Because the struggles Hillary lived through are no longer just her story, they are now part of America's history. They are part of our story. And when you undertake your presidential run, your story will be something we recognize, something familiar.

★

And here I am, writing my story in hopes that my words can make a difference for you. After the campaign ended, I thought about writing a book. I wondered if my story would resonate only where it intersected with someone else's interesting life. Initially I was advised that if I didn't have something juicy to share about Hillary, there wouldn't be interest in me. (By the way, there aren't any juicy things to share about Hillary because she's a simple and serious person.)

I also learned that John Heilemann and Mark Halperin were going to do a third *Game Change* book. The original *Game Change* was written about the 2008 campaign and had been hugely successful. They had followed it up with one about the 2012 campaign and now planned a third about the highly dramatic last forty-five days of the 2016 race. A frustrating fact of the campaign staffer's life is that the campaign books that usually sell the best and are given the most credence are the books written by the people who observed the campaign but weren't a part of it. When you aren't there, living the day-to-day, you can't tell the whole truth.

John Heilemann got in touch in the spring of 2017 to ask if I would participate. I equivocated. Even though I had given up the idea of writing a book, it still didn't sit right with me that someone else would tell our story.

After a few weeks, I decided I would cooperate with them. I knew it would be a successful book, had an HBO movie deal attached to it, and would be treated as the definitive account of the campaign. When they wrote the original *Game Change* in 2008, I didn't participate and Elizabeth Edwards got pretty well beaten up as a consequence. I didn't want the same thing to happen to Hillary. If the book was going to matter, I wanted to make sure it was true.

I told John I was ready to talk with him and started a series of meetings with him in the late spring. Our last meeting was in October shortly before their book deal blew up over Mark Halperin's allegations. In that October meeting, John told me I had spent a total of seventeen hours with him, and sometimes him and Mark, answering questions. Each of those hours was exhausting. The periods I sat with him didn't feel like interviews, they felt like "sessions." They were emotional and draining. It was two to three hours of answering questions about something I no longer had any ability to do anything about. It wasn't John's fault; it was just an awful process. I always left feeling depleted and powerless.

Then one day, I realized I was not powerless. I shut out other voices from my head and forced myself to acknowledge that, regardless of what anyone else may think, I believed I had a powerful story to tell and I was going to figure out how to tell it. Once I had the courage to say this out loud, I learned I wasn't the only one who thought I had something valuable to say. Everyone I told about my book idea, from Hillary to Elizabeth's family to John Heilemann, also agreed. I realized then how wrong I was to doubt myself, and you should too. And so I have told my story to help you and every woman who knows she can lead but is uncertain about how to use her voice.

With the #MeToo movement, 2017 was a watershed year for women telling their own stories as victims of sexual assault and harassment. It was nothing less than a revolution. Their accounts are unflinching, powerful, and, most important, told in their own voices. To those who ask why they waited so long to tell their stories, I say the real question is, what gave them the courage to tell their stories even now?

Each of these women had more to risk than to gain by telling her story, and did so anyway. Each of them saw a reason to believe her words could make a difference, and they have. Merely through the power of their words, these women have laid bare the true extent of sexually inappropriate male behavior in our culture, which in turn is forcing a zero-tolerance approach to the problem. These women are writing a brand-new chapter in American history and radically changing the balance of power in the workplace, simply because they knew what had happened to them was unjust and decided that their own voices gave them the power to right an injustice.

We have learned to stop searching for where we fit into history because we are writing our own story.

Chapter Eight

UNDEFEATED

Even when you lose,
refuse to be defeated.

*I*t's Saturday, September 10, 2016. The Doral Arrowwood hotel in Westchester County, New York. It was near the Clintons' home and was the hotel we used for debate-prep meetings throughout the campaign. I come in late to debate prep. The room is silent when I walk in and stays silent for four full minutes. I count them. Four minutes is a long time. Things aren't going well.

I gather the topic is why our economic message isn't breaking through more. We move on to discuss the Trump campaign's stepped-up attacks against Hillary. It's been a few days since Steve Bannon's appointment as CEO of the Trump campaign and their declaration of a "scorched earth" strategy to drive down enthusiasm for Hillary by relentlessly attacking her. I understand the Trump campaign also hopes its attacks will drive down the morale of our own campaign team, and in that moment they are succeeding in doing so. That gets me mad. After all our campaign has survived, we can't let the Trump team deflate us like this.

It's my nature to try to see a terrible situation in the best possible light. Most people would look at the Trump campaign's new team and strategy and be chilled. I choose to see a frustrated group who has been trying to tear Hillary Clinton down for the last twenty-five years and hasn't been able to do it.

I am still not fully recovered from my own illness that landed me in the hospital. I speak anyway. I go off on a tear. An epic tear. I recount in detail all the attacks Hillary has had thrown at her in her adult life. This takes a while. I go on to what she has faced in this election—emails, eleven-hour Benghazi testimony, an FBI investigation, WikiLeaks, a grueling Democratic primary, seventeen people (fifteen Republican candidates and two in the Democratic primary) attacking her every single day. Hillary Clinton was subjected to more attacks than any presidential candidate in our history. Those attacks would have killed a weaker candidate. No one but her could have survived all of this.

"Madam Secretary," I say, "do not see all these attacks and get discouraged. Look at them and marvel at how frustrated these Republicans are that they can't take you down. Think about what a miracle it is that you are still standing.

"It is a *fucking miracle*," I conclude, my voice shaking.

Silence in the room.

She nods. And for the first time that day, I see her give a slight smile.

I have processed and accepted a lot of what

happened in this election. The one thing I haven't been able to accept is that her attackers finally succeeded in defeating her. I just don't believe that's true.

Whether or not you are defeated is your choice. Defeated is when you fail to look your opponent in the face and call them out on their hate or lies. Defeated is when you cower when attacked. Defeated is when you give up the fight. Worse, defeated is when you give up hope. Hillary never cowered in the face of attacks or failed to call out hate. And after she lost, she refused to stop fighting for the issues and people she cared about. Hillary may have lost this election, but she refused to be defeated.

I talked with Hillary during the campaign about how she makes it through tough times. She said she gets up every day, focuses on what she has to do that day, does the best she can on that day, and then gets up the next day and does it again. Pretty simple. Takes a lot of fortitude, though. She has plenty of that.

It is an empowering and liberating lesson. I hope it is one you take to heart, Madam President. There will be many times in your career when you will be told you have been beaten. When that happens, think of the stories I am about to tell you. These people faced devastating moments when life told them they lost, but they refused to be defeated. They mourned their losses, then they dug deep to figure out a way to keep going and do what they could do to make their lives matter.

Elizabeth Edwards always managed to find a way to make her life matter. Elizabeth was the wife of my onetime boss and presidential candidate, Senator John Edwards. I first met her at their home when I came to interview to be John's press secretary in late 2002. We hit it off immediately and remained close friends until her death in 2010. We both grew up in navy families, came from an Italian-American background, and shared a tendency to get pretty sassy. Elizabeth was one of the smartest people I have ever known and certainly had the quickest wit. The best way I can describe the special talents she had is to say that she lived life with enormous ambition on a small scale. She was very knowledgeable about policy and cared a great deal about the world around her, but where she placed all her ambition and where she created real magic was in the comparatively small-scale lives of her family and friends. She once actually captained an effort to grow a golf course for her son and his friends to wear as a Halloween costume. She soaked eighteen boys' sweat suits in water and grass seed, hung the suits over hangers covered in plastic dry-cleaning bags to simulate a greenhouse, and grew grass suits for them all to wear. That is ambition.

Elizabeth honestly believed she had all of life's answers. Other than preventing or undoing death, she thought there was a solution to any problem you encountered. Anyone who didn't understand that it was possible was frustrating and dull in her view. To be clear, Elizabeth thought that *Elizabeth* had the answers to all of life's problems. This was not a skill that she believed extended to everyone. But, thankfully for those of us in her life, she was there to tell us what we needed to do.

Elizabeth endured a lot of heartache. Most notably, her sixteen-year-old son, Wade, was killed in a car accident in 1996. She said she had imagined her mind before Wade's death as a crowded chalkboard upon which she scrawled everything she worried about, cared about, and needed or wanted to do. It was completely filled, every inch of space taken up, covered in little scribbles of chalk. When Wade died, everything on the board was erased, the entire board wiped clean. She let it sit empty for a long time after that. Once your board has been wiped clean, you want to be very deliberate about what you put on it.

When Elizabeth first told me about her chalkboard, I thought I understood. It made sense. Don't sweat the small stuff. Focus on the things that matter, like your children. I saw it as a call for each individual to be deliberate about the choices in his or her life in order to live the most rewarding life.

I stood before my own blank slate in November 2016 and realized that I had failed to see the deeper purpose in Elizabeth's new board. It's not just that life is fleeting or you want to be deliberate in your choices because so little is within your control. *It's not about making sure your life is rewarding—it's about making sure your life matters.* You want whatever time you have on this earth to matter. I should have understood fifteen years ago that's what she meant. People of goodwill, working together, can make a difference. That was one of her life mantras. That's the lesson that was always at the top of her chalkboard.

She stood before her blank chalkboard and thought hard about what would matter to her and bring joy back into her life. She decided to have two more children, and Emma Claire and Jack brought her enormous happiness and fulfillment.

She refused to live a life without joy. For her that would have been accepting defeat.

Later, she would become sick with cancer. Twice. She endured an unfaithful husband in front of the world. She wanted it to be known about her that she "stood in the storm, and when the wind did not blow her away, she adjusted her sails." I was with her for a lot of those difficult days of cancer and infidelity. While it is true that she adjusted her sails, I know she won't mind me telling you that she also did plenty of howling into the wind over the pain of it all. Feeling the pain is part of standing in the storm. You shouldn't try to escape it or suppress the grief the pain causes. The pain isn't what will defeat you. What matters is what you choose to do once the storm passes.

On the night of Wednesday, December 1, 2010, Elizabeth called me from her home in Chapel Hill to let me know that she had stopped treatments for her cancer. She would die soon.

I asked her how long she had. She said weeks—maybe two, maybe eight. Not long. I asked her if she thought she would be with Wade after she passed. She said she did. Neither one of us had much to say after that. Because it's not just the friend of the sick person who doesn't know what to say in the face of this kind of news. The person facing death also doesn't know what to say. She hadn't been through this, either. Still, I felt very close to Elizabeth in that moment. I knew she didn't expect some magic words of comfort from me. My presence was enough.

After some minutes of silence, she told me that she had happy news, too. Her eldest daughter, Cate, had gotten engaged to her beau, Trevor, over the Thanksgiving weekend. They are two of my favorite people on the planet, and I was very happy to hear this news. But it forced me to envision the world in which Cate's wedding would happen and know that Elizabeth would not be in it. The closeness I had felt to Elizabeth just minutes before started to slip away. It seemed to me she was already fading from this world.

I was scheduled to fly from Washington to Raleigh the next day to testify in front of the grand jury that was hearing a case against her husband. Elizabeth did not know this. I had not talked with her for months. I had been interviewed by the Justice Department several times over the course of the last six months about their investigation of John. I just couldn't bring myself to talk to her during that period, although I now regret those months I was not around to be her friend.

I told her that I was going to be in North Carolina the next day and why. She said she was sorry I had to go through the grand jury testimony. I told her I would spend the night in Chapel Hill and come see her on Friday. I hoped when I saw her we could plan one last trip with some of our other girlfriends to visit T.J.Maxx.

Elizabeth was a beautiful woman who on most days cared little about how she looked or what she wore. Nevertheless, she loved to shop, though truth be told, she had terrible taste in clothes. If she ever drove past a T.J.Maxx without stopping, it wasn't when she was in my company. Sometimes she would buy something for me after having shopped there on her own. The clothes she purchased for me can only be described as "frocks." Always weird smock-like shirts or dresses in a mismatch of patterns. Just awful. They were gifts for me but she also always wanted me to see how little she'd paid for them. "Look!" she would cry, showing me the price tag. "Can you believe what a good deal I got on this?!" And I would say, "Why, yes, Elizabeth. Yes, I can." Once—and only once—she purchased a very beautiful white Cynthia Rowley cardigan sweater at a T.J.Maxx in New Hampshire. She is wearing it on the paperback edition of her book *Saving Graces*. It is my favorite picture of her. She made me promise that when she died I would make sure the press used the photo of her in the Cynthia Rowley sweater. I kept my promise.

So, I hoped one last T.J.Maxx trip with her and maybe a stop at Sonic Drive-In (her idea of a perfect day) would be possible. But when I saw her that Friday morning, I realized it was too late. She was alert and very much herself but already restricted to her bed. I stayed for a few hours. It felt like one of our normal visits, our conversation a mix of the everyday and the big stuff. We talked about whether she was scared. She was relieved to tell me that she was not scared to die. She was at peace and knew she would soon see Wade. I was very relieved to hear that. She asked me about Jim and what my stepdaughters, Lizz and Kat, were up to. She fretted about how the UNC basketball team would fare against Kentucky that weekend. (UNC won.) We talked about redecorating my home and she had some views on paint and furniture color combinations. I took her advice.

Eventually, I asked her if she wanted to share some kind of goodbye message for all the people, mostly women, who had derived so much strength and grace from her books. I said it could be pretty distressing for some of her admirers to just learn one day that she was gone with no final words from her to assure them that she was fine at the end, and that those also facing a terminal disease would be fine, too. She agreed and asked me to take notes for her on what she wanted to say. I left to catch my flight with a promise to come back the next week to see her. I gave her a hug and walked out of her room. She called to me on my way out of her house: "Love you, JP!"

"Love you, Elizabeth!" I called back.

When I got to the airport, I typed up her notes and sent them in an email to her and her brother, Jay Anania. The next day John Edwards called me to say the doctors thought she could die that night. Christina Reynolds, my friend who had worked on the Edwards campaigns with me and also been very close to Elizabeth, and I flew down to be there. When I landed in Raleigh, it was snowing, something that had not happened in Raleigh in many years. The night had an otherworldly quality. When we got to the house, Elizabeth was still alive but could no longer converse. I was very grateful for the time she and I had the day before.

On Monday, Cate posted the goodbye message on Elizabeth's Facebook page. Elizabeth died the next day. I continue to find inspiration in this passage from her post: "I have found that in the simple act of living with hope, and in the daily effort to have a positive impact in the world, the days I do have are made all the more meaningful and precious."

I thought of Elizabeth's message when I met the Mothers of the Movement during Hillary's campaign. They are African American mothers who lost their children to gun violence and/or at the hands of the police. As they say, they were turning their mourning into a movement. Geneva Reed-Veal, Gwen Carr, Sybrina Fulton, Lucia McBath—these women have so much courage and grace.

They are struggling to look beyond their loss, which in most cases had happened because of the color of their child's skin, to seek justice and foster more understanding with the hope that other families don't suffer the same pain they have. They speak of their work in the Movement as a way to continue to parent the children they lost. They have found a way to make sure their children's lives, and their own lives, continue to matter. These mothers may be heartbroken, but they are not defeated.

I thought of Elizabeth's message when I met Mark Barden, father of Daniel Barden, who was killed in the Newtown shooting. I personally have never seen a more devastated soul on God's earth than a parent who lost a child in Newtown. Yet Mark, in his devastation, works tirelessly to do all he can to fight gun violence and continue to parent Daniel's memory. He has made sure Daniel's life, and Mark's own time on this earth, continue to matter. While Mark may be heartbroken, he is not defeated.

And I thought of Elizabeth's message when my own sister Dana called to tell me that she had early-onset Alzheimer's. It was a shocking diagnosis, but the way Dana decided she was going to handle it was not at all surprising. She told all of her family members that we were to see her diagnosis as a blessing. It would allow her to retire early. It would motivate our family to spend more time together than we otherwise would have. She may have fewer days on the earth than she wanted, but she would make sure the days she did have left mattered. She made good on her promise and spent her remaining time trying to have a positive impact on the lives of the people around her every day. As her world got smaller, Dana held tight to a mantra that defined the elements of her life: "May I be safe and loved. May I be happy and healthy. May I be kind and caring. May I know that all is well." The disease took away many years of her life. But instead of focusing on what had been lost, Dana redefined her universe, stripping away all the excess and embracing a life lived solely to maximize its harmony with and benevolent influence on those around her. She was not defeated. She made me very proud to be her sister.

Madam President, I hope you never know the heartache of a lost child or a devastating illness. But like all of us, you will face moments of tragedy and loss and be tested by them. When you fall short or the country gets discouraged, look beyond the loss before you to see what else is possible. You may need to set your sights farther in the future, dig a little deeper, and find the strength to keep going. Don't fall into the trap of thinking that any cause or battle you take on has to be won in order to have been worth doing. Believe that the effort you put into something that really matters to you is its own reward, whether your efforts succeed or not. If your cause is right, you will eventually prevail. Till then, stay true to your principles; if you will yourself to fight on, you will never be defeated.

Chapter Nine

BOUND TOGETHER

We are bound together.
Now we need to unite.

This story ends where it started, election night 2016. It is the story of a national reckoning that was a long time coming. It's a cautionary tale with an important lesson about the country you are to lead—that Americans truly are bound together, even when they're not united.

On this night, I see for the first time the CNN chyron: DONALD TRUMP ELECTED US PRESIDENT. He is giving his victory speech. I find it odd that CNN felt the need to specify "US President." In that moment, I also see:

Myself on my couch in Alexandria, Virginia, on November 7, 2000: CNN chyron: GEORGE BUSH ELECTED PRESIDENT.

Myself in our Columbus boiler room of the Ohio Kerry campaign headquarters on November 3, 2004: CNN chyron: GEORGE BUSH RE-ELECTED PRESIDENT.

Myself at the BBC studio in Washington, DC, on November 4, 2008: CNN chyron: BARACK OBAMA ELECTED PRESIDENT.

Myself in the Roosevelt Room of the White House on November 6, 2012: CNN chyron: BARACK OBAMA RE-ELECTED PRESIDENT.

Madam President, in that instant, I tried to fathom how each of those nights had been leading us to this one. I tried to fathom the frustrations that had been building, the fissures solidifying into divisions and taking hold in America. I could not process it all in that moment, but this much was clear to me: America would have to endure a reckoning.

I had hoped that the election itself would be

this reckoning. It was clear by the fall of 2015 that this election cycle was something different. It wasn't going to be simply a "change election" or a referendum on Obama or even an election about the economy. It was about what kind of country we are going to be. You could feel that all these frustrations that had been simmering underground for a long time had roiled to the surface. My hope was that the campaign would be the vessel through which America would face this reckoning, select Hillary over Trump, progress over regression, love over hate, and we would move on reassured that America had some of its core principles tested and chose the right path. By three a.m. on Wednesday, it was becoming clearer the election was not going to be the end of this battle. It was just the beginning.

There were moments along the way that hinted that this reckoning was coming. Like Friday, June 26, 2015. It had been a remarkable couple of days. On Thursday, the United States Supreme

Court upheld the Affordable Care Act. On Friday, it ruled on the right of gay people to marry in this country. In the wake of the terrible race-motivated shootings at the Emanuel AME Church in Charleston, it looked like the Confederate flag might finally be removed from the grounds of the South Carolina State House. And on Friday afternoon, after speaking emotionally about the gay marriage decision in the Rose Garden that morning, President Obama broke out into an impromptu rendition of "Amazing Grace" at the Charleston memorial service for the nine people killed in that shooting.

That Friday night, I took a walk around my Fort Greene neighborhood. I couldn't stop smiling. It wasn't just me—all of Brooklyn was in a good mood, celebrating the payoff of decades upon decades of struggle that had gone into making the progress represented in that one week. I took time to think through all the years of effort it had taken to make these wins possible—the health care fight started at the time of FDR, LGBTQ rights before that, and we had fought a war more than 150 years ago about that flag.

Even as I sat among the happy Brooklynites celebrating love being love, I knew there were people in America who wouldn't welcome any of this—upholding Obamacare, gay marriage, the loss of the display of the Confederate flag—as progress. Rather, they would look upon this week and feel alienated in their own country. That's a sad and terrible way to have to live. I thought of Donald Trump, who had announced his candidacy for president two weeks prior with a divisive speech that painted a picture of America in decline. The frustration felt in America was not limited to these three areas. It was growing everywhere. *Boy,* I thought. *We could be in for one hell of a backlash.*

That first summer of the campaign we had our hands full with our own primary but watched what was happening with the rise of Trump on the Republican side with an equal mix of schadenfreude and unease, as the Republican Party seemed intent on nominating the most polarizing candidate imaginable. We saw that Trump was striking a chord with voters in a way you rarely see in campaigns and breaking all the rules of politics as he did it.

By the fall of 2015, Hillary and Bill Clinton understood there was a deep and disturbing disaffection at work in the electorate. Initially I thought, or at least hoped, they were wrong. They aired these concerns in earnest at one of our first debate prep sessions in the fall of 2015. We were working in a ballroom of the Doral Arrowwood. Both the Clintons were there and sharing how disconcerted they felt by what they saw from voters on the campaign trail—both on the Democratic side and in the Republican primary. Anger, alienation, a dearth of hope. It troubled them greatly. They had not ever seen anything like it. It was pretty sobering to be told by these two that we were experiencing something in politics that even they had not experienced.

I told them I thought they were misreading the trajectory voters were on. I believed that 2010 had been the year of true voter disaffection. Because Hillary was secretary of state at that time, and therefore not involved in the midterm elections, the Clintons hadn't experienced them the way they were experiencing this election. That was the year of anger, I said. 2012 was better. 2016 was seven years on from the recession, so voter dissatisfaction would be further eased.

No, they were right. 2016 was something different.

Another debate prep, February 2016: A different room at the same Doral Arrowwood. The same players. We had lost New Hampshire the night before by twenty-two points. It was one of the worst days of the campaign. This time I just listened when the Clintons aired their fears. I knew they were right. They had both re-read *The True Believer* by Eric Hoffer and told us all we should read it. Hoffer wrote it in the 1950s about the rise of mass movements and authoritarian leaders. The Clintons feared there were parallels between the story laid out in the book and what we were living through in America in 2016.

Hoffer postulates that people's frustration doesn't come out during a crisis—like a war or times of extreme poverty. During those times, people are focused on surviving. They have purpose and don't have the luxury or inclination to rebel. Frustration comes later, when circumstances in a country are improving, but not fast enough. Or not for everyone. Or when people are angered and unsettled by the lack of purpose they feel now compared to the worth they felt their lives had when they were part of a larger struggle during the time of crisis. It is at this time that they gravitate toward dangerous leaders, those who lead by pitting people against each other, who have no coherent agenda but attract people by offering them a sense of reflected glory, who sound and act just like Donald Trump.

I read the book. It was filled with stories of the kind of things you think can't happen in America. But the Clintons were right. I saw a lot of parallels to what we were experiencing in America in 2016.

After all, our country had been through very trying times. We had faced enormous change, stress, and disruption in the last fifteen years. I used to think about it when I worked in the Obama White House. I knew we would look back at the first part of the twenty-first century as a time of enormous upheaval. September 11, two wars, the Great Recession, enormous demographic changes, ever-growing economic inequality, a dramatic tech revolution, the digital economy, climate change.

What about me? What part of this do I own, Madam President? Some friends kindly said to me after the election that they hoped I didn't blame myself for the loss. The first few times I heard this I was a little taken aback. Blame myself? Don't worry, I didn't. I knew I did everything I could. I left it all on the field.

Still, I was part of a political class that thought we alone understood the rules of politics and everyone had to play by those rules, as established by us. After a while, the public is ready to believe that politics really is just a game, that none of it really matters. They think their democracy doesn't have anything to do with them. It's a game set up and managed by a handful of people in Washington.

Anyway, I guess the joke's on me. Donald Trump violated just about every rule there was in politics and won. He defied gravity. Disruption had come to my industry the way it had to so many others. Nothing made sense to me anymore. Right. This is how the man who worked in coal his whole life and now can't find a decent job feels. This is how the cabdriver who has been run out of business by Uber feels. This is how everyone feels whose life plan was blown up by some unexpected and confounding force.

I have accepted that the days of being able to predict how our politics will play out are over. I have also accepted that's how it should be. A small number of people in Washington shouldn't be able to predict—let alone orchestrate—what our entire democracy is going to do. That paradigm had to topple. It needed to topple.

It's why I shake my head when my friends in politics talk about how the political parties in Washington have to figure out what their national message is. As if things are going to go back to "normal" after the 2016 elections. As if Washington types can still control outcomes. As if that world hasn't already blown up. That's not how this is going down. The rebirth will come from the ground up or it won't come at all.

During the course of the campaign, I had the chance to go to most states in America. The upheaval was happening everywhere, across every demographic. We were overdue for a reckoning of grievances, and we lived in a new world where people have more platforms and means than ever to express those grievances.

Madam President, it is important for you to know that I have never thought this reckoning necessarily spells doom for America. It could, if we don't figure out a way to bridge our differences, but I am hopeful because I see a unifying thread linking these groups of frustrated Americans. They all thought America could be better than it was in that moment. That America was not living up to her values. The world was changing fast, both economically and socially, and it seemed like America wasn't able to adjust, as it always has in the past. To many on both sides of the ideological spectrum, it felt like our political leadership was only making the divisions in our country worse.

The two sides were certainly very far apart, but the bottom line is that everyone expected better of this country. To me, that is common ground upon which to build, and because of that, I find this reckoning reassuring to some degree. It shows that we really are all in this together. The pain one group feels in America can't stay isolated forever. Eventually it will spill out and we will all feel it, because we are connected to each other. The charge now is to move from understanding that we are bound together to choosing to be united. To live up to our best values so everyone feels like they are part of this country and can see the path for how they can succeed here. To build enough understanding among all of us that a gain for one isn't seen as a loss by another.

What's the lesson for you to make sure we don't allow this kind of disaffection and corrosive alienation to take hold again? Be a president for all of America—the people who vote for you and the ones who don't. Listen to everyone's concerns, and even when you can't agree with people, make sure they know you have heard them, that you understand their point of view, and that there is a place for everyone at the table.

Sounds like a good job for a woman.

And a good place for my letter to end. The lessons I shared are hard-earned and the advice I offer is well-meaning. I hope they boost your confidence and make you appreciate the breadth of talents you will bring to this job.

Frankly, I am surprised to find myself advising you and other women on how we can reach equality with men. I spent most of my life thinking we were already there. We are not. For me, it took living through Hillary's bewildering campaign and processing the factors behind her loss to understand that we are not there. For other women, it was the promotion that never came, or the umpteenth time a male colleague was lauded for an idea that had been ignored when a woman suggested it earlier, or the most recent time you were told you are a good sport for staying later than all the men and being the one who did all "the real work" that showed us we are not there. Some women I know—particularly women who are black or brown, less wealthy, or older than I am—have always understood we have not reached equality.

I am just one woman. I can only offer lessons learned from my own experiences and I know I have lived a life of privilege that made being fearless in the workplace an easier and relatively risk-free thing for me to do. Still, I ask you and all the women reading this to embrace the lessons I have told you here, look at the work that still lays before us, and be inspired, not discouraged. A better world than we have ever known is in the offing—a world where women are able to achieve all we seek to achieve and everyone is better off for it. It's exciting. So when disaster strikes and the unimaginable happens, don't allow yourself to be defeated. Look around the new world you are in and imagine what else may be possible for you there.

Speak up. Cry if you are moved to do so. Don't stifle your emotions or your ambitions.

Don't wait for permission or an invitation or expect to find your place in someone else's story. Jump in to whatever it is you want to do. Embrace your age—whatever it may be—and all that your experience and perspective give you to teach the rest of us. Try seeing your male colleagues as partners, not masters. And if men refuse to see you as an equal and you aren't able to beat them or join them—then just ignore them. Don't let anyone, man or woman, decide if you matter. You know you do.

You already hold all the wisdom, strength, and confidence you need to accomplish whatever it is you want to do. What has held us back before is merely our collective inability to imagine what is possible for us to do. The talent and ability have always been there.

The generations of women before us, who made countless, mostly anonymous, sacrifices in the struggle for equality, paved the way for real change. In spite of the long odds against them, they went after the impossible. It is up to us—the women in America today—to finish the job. It's a thrilling challenge. Go show us what a woman leading us in this new world looks like. We can't wait to see.

With love and admiration,

Jennifer

ACKNOWLEDGMENTS

First and foremost, thank you to Robin Sproul of Javelin for pushing me to write a book. I would not have had the courage or platform to do it if not for her encouragement. Robin, Matt Latimer, and Keith Urbahn at Javelin all convinced me that I could, and should, write this book. They approached this project with innovative thinking and commitment and I am forever grateful to each of them.

I now understand why all authors offer such profuse thanks to their editor. Gretchen Young at

Grand Central Publishing saw the possibility of this book before I did and was willing to take a chance on a first-time author with an aggressive deadline. I am so thankful to her for her never-failing support, ideas, enthusiasm, and energy. I cannot imagine a more generous, patient, and helpful editor. Thank you.

A number of people in my life gave me invaluable support and encouragement during this project, and I am grateful to them all. Thank you to Laurene Powell Jobs, Stacey Rubin, Neera Tanden, Valerie Jarrett, John Podesta, Minyon Moore, Emily Bromberg and Stephen Silverman, Daniella Gibbs Leger, Denis McDonough, Jennifer Shelton, Jenni LeCompte, and Joel Johnson.

The Hillary sisterhood persists. We continue to love, support, and prop up each other. Thanks to Helen Brosnan, Crystal Carson, Brynne Craig, Adrienne Elrod, Maya Harris, Xochitl Hinojosa, Sara Latham, Amanda Littman, Lori Lodes, Jenna Lowenstein, Lucy MacIntosh, Zerlina

Maxwell, Jess MacIntosh, Jess Morales Rocketto, Olivia Raisner, Christina Reynolds, and Kristina Schake for the support this past year.

★

To my extended Elizabeth family, Jay Anania and Jackie Soeher, Nancy Anania, Glenn Bergenfield, Cate Edwards, David Ginsberg, Andrea Purse, Ellis Roberts, and Trevor Upham, I simply say, "You know."

To my own extended family, I am grateful for, and awed by, our collective love, strength, wisdom, and dedication. They are my parents, John and Nancy Palmieri. My sisters and brothers-in-law, who have always been my role models and nurtured me: Scott Evans, Misty Keown, Beth Palmieri, Jim and Lisa Shannon. Nell Bieger, Ingrid Moss, and Lucy Trent, who remain a part of our family. My stepdaughters, Lizz and Kat Lyons, and my nieces and nephews, Johnny, Nick, and

Rebecca Drago, and Patrick, Ashley, Casey, and Caroline Shannon, who give me hope for the future. And, finally, my husband, Jim Lyons, whose heart, brilliance, and imagination have given me so much happiness and fulfillment, and whose love sustains me.

About the Author

Jennifer Palmieri was the director of communications for Hillary Clinton's 2016 presidential campaign. Prior to that position, she served as the White House communications director for President Barack Obama. She was also the national press secretary for the 2004 John Edwards presidential campaign and for the Democratic Party in 2002. She frequently appears as a political commentator on television and radio outlets. Jennifer and her husband reside in Maryland.